BROADCAST YOUR INNER CHAMPION

A JOURNEY OF SELF-REMEMBRANCE... AND IMPACT!

STEVE BERLACK

Copyright © 2014 Steve Berlack.

All rights reserved. No part of this book may be reproduced, stored, or transmitted by any means—whether auditory, graphic, mechanical, or electronic—without written permission of both publisher and author, except in the case of brief excerpts used in critical articles and reviews. Unauthorized reproduction of any part of this work is illegal and is punishable by law.

Cover photo by: Erica L. Spruill

ISBN: 978-1-4834-2058-5 (sc)
ISBN: 978-1-4834-2057-8 (e)

Because of the dynamic nature of the Internet, any web addresses or links contained in this book may have changed since publication and may no longer be valid. The views expressed in this work are solely those of the author and do not necessarily reflect the views of the publisher, and the publisher hereby disclaims any responsibility for them.

Any people depicted in stock imagery provided by Thinkstock are models, and such images are being used for illustrative purposes only. Certain stock imagery © Thinkstock.

Lulu Publishing Services rev. date: 11/26/2014

Contents

Prologue: The Berlack Method to Broadcasting vii

Chapter 1	Self-Awareness 1
Chapter 2	Faith 29
Chapter 3	Attitude & Success 51
Chapter 4	Spiritual Connection & Responsibility 77
Chapter 5	Cultural Connection 95
Chapter 6	Achieving with Others (Team Building) 109
Chapter 7	Relationship Building (Personal) 129
Chapter 8	Parenting 151
Chapter 9	Leadership Development 179
Chapter 10	Community Impact 193

Epilogue: Connect the Dots…and Broadcast! 237
Thanks & Acknowledgements 251
About The Author 255

Prologue:
The Berlack Method to Broadcasting

> "I cannot help you shine your light by talking about your light. I can only help you shine your light by shining mine." – Steve Berlack

"Who are you?" That's the first question of the first workshop of The Berlack Method Personal Development Training Series. I have asked that question hundreds, if not thousands of times over the years, and I've asked it of children, adolescents, young adults and the elderly. I've asked it of people all over the country from various cultural, ethnic and racial backgrounds, and of both genders. One thing has become clear. This is an exceedingly difficult and complicated question to answer. At first, that may seem counter-intuitive. It is, after all, a simple question. But it is precisely the fundamental nature of the question that makes it so difficult to answer.

For example, almost every time I ask the question, an audience member's initial response is to tell me his/her name. At first thought, that makes sense. We carry our names with us from birth, and they are our primary identifiers. We cling to our names as hallmarks of our identity. Although I agree that our names *can* be that hallmark, I've found that something is usually missing between the act of stating our names and understanding what our names represent. For instance, when I hit my audience with the idea that their names tell me how they're called, but not who they are, they're stumped. It usually goes something like this:

Me: "Who are you?"
Audience member: "My name is Joe Smith." *To the reader: what does this tell you about the audience member?*

Me: "That just tells me what to call you. Let me try again: who are you?"
Audience member: <<silence>>

I've found that many people are stumped because they know neither the meaning nor the spirit of their names. For instance, my name is Steven Bernard Berlack. "Steven" means crowned one, while "Bernard" means strong, brave bear. "Berlack" is the name shortened at Ellis Island by the immigration officer who couldn't pronounce my great-great grandfather's surname. A youthful Prussian Jewish immigrant, he hardly had the wherewithal to protest. Therefore, if anyone asks me who I am, I not only tell them my name, I tell them what it means, and, more importantly, that my knowledge of what it means impacts me in that I conduct myself as a man of royalty, and that I see myself as strong enough spiritually and mentally, and brave enough by birthright to overcome any obstacles that come my way. My strength and bravery are buttressed by the family history told to me by my grandparents as I bounced on their knees as a boy.

It is because I am conscious to live in the spirit of my name, both in its meaning and history, that I am aware of who I am. And it is because I am aware that I have, to the degree that you may judge, been both blessed and successful. And so, dear reader, I ask the question of you: "who are you?" Whether you can answer the question swiftly and with detail, or you find yourself silent and wondering, this book, like the personal development workshops that inspired it, is designed to help you explore, identify and broadcast your answer.

THIS ISN'T A BOOK SO MUCH AS IT'S A JOURNEY TO REMEMBER WHO YOU ARE.

I have become convinced that we spend our lives not *discovering* who we are, but *remembering* who we are. The difference is nuanced and subtle, yet sharply distinct and clear. I was inspired to believe this idea by Jeremiah 1:5 - *"Before I formed you in the womb I knew you, before you were born I set you apart; I appointed you as a prophet to the nations."* What this says to me is that there is much more to our lives than what we see, touch and feel during our lifetimes. We are more than that. Because we are more, there are innumerable subtleties and nuances we must explore to fully answer the question: "who are you?" It was because of this idea that I wrote "Dust of the Earth," which you'll find in the Chapter *Self-Awareness*. As you read the chapters in this book, you will be challenged to explore who you are, think about whether or not you are culturally and spiritually connected to others, what responsibility you bear for this connection, and how this knowledge can lead you to positively impact those around you.

There are ten workshops in The Berlack Method, and ten themed chapters of "Broadcast Your Inner Champion" that correspond to them. They are, in order:

* Self – Awareness
* Faith
* Attitude & Success
* Spiritual Connection & Responsibility
* Cultural Connection
* Achieving with Others
* Relationship Building
* Parenting
* Leadership Development
* Community Impact

You may have noticed that the themes are ordered to challenge you in precisely the way I mentioned above. The purpose of this book is to massage you into asking and answering, chapter by chapter, the following questions:

1. What do you think about this theme?
2. Why do you think the way you do?
3. What must you explore to discover what you think and why?
    a. Daily life challenges
        i. Attitudes of family, friends and general society
        ii. Finances
        iii. Love and relationships
        iv. Career

How did all of life's challenges impact how you thought and acted? How does knowing this change how you may think and act in the future?

If successful, this book will not only challenge you to explore the questions above, it will move you through the process of becoming truly self-aware, to fully understanding your perception of your connection to and responsibility for others, and ultimately to impacting others in a meaningful and positive way. You will be, for all intents and purposes, broadcasting your inner champion.

A WORD ABOUT FAITH

The second question I ask in the Self-Awareness workshop is: "To Whom Do You Belong?" The reason I have for asking that? Simple: I've never known anyone who fully explored who they are without examining the spirit. While this book does not espouse a particular religion, it unabashedly explores the role of God in our lives. There have been more than a few who tried to poke holes in The Berlack Method by mentioning that they're not Christian, or that they don't believe in God in any form. My answer to them is simple: "That's fine." While walking your journey of self-remembrance, it's not important that you believe as I do, or even agree that there is a God. What's important is that you understand and can articulate *what* you believe and *why*. I was having a debate about God when the words quoted at the beginning of this book hit me like a bolt of lightening. I'm not a Christian because I have all the answers about God, I'm a Christian because I have faith in Him.

In fact, the biggest obstacle I faced in giving my life to Christ was the battle waged within me about having to "figure it all out." The intellectual in me was never satisfied unless I "knew" the correct answers about God, Jesus, religion, etc. However, as I grew older, I continued to dream about my spirituality (you'll read more about that in the epilogue), and I received countless signs and confirmations about my relationship with God and my purpose. Finally, one day, while talking to a good friend about this, she looked me in the eye and asked: "How many signs do you need?" And that was that. I fell to the floor, prostrated and crying. I've consciously given my life to Him ever since. Notice I didn't say "I've been a Christian ever since," because that takes me back to Jeremiah 1:5. I've always been who I am. I'm just on a journey to remember.

No one ever convinced me to become a Christian. The best they could do was show me who they were, and allow me the space to learn from them what I could and put away the rest. This book is not designed to convince you of anything, (how could it?), but to shine the light of my experiences for you in a safe, non-judgmental way that allows you to explore your own ideas about spirituality, religion, etc. Your answer to "to whom do you belong?" is a reflection of your journey, not mine. And your answer is safe here.

A WORD ON POLITICS

You'll notice, especially in Chapter 10, that I feel free to articulate my political leanings. I do so in the same spirit in which I discuss my faith. You may find that you disagree with my thoughts on all things political, and my answer to you would be..."that's fine." I make my points not because I'm trying to convince you of anything, but because my political views are a reflection of my experience…my light. I can only shine my light. If you disagree, then please know that the same principles applied to faith in this book are also applied to politics. So feel free! Shout at the book about why I'm *so* wrong and about how crazy I am! (I'd actually love to see that)! Shine *your* light! If you're like me, you'll find that openly articulating your views within a healthy, respectful debate enriches and crystalizes them in a powerful way.

And what's wrong with that?

HOW THIS BOOK IS SET UP

After the prologue, "Broadcast Your Inner Champion" is divided into ten chapters that align with the themes of The Berlack Method listed earlier. Although there is a specific order to The Method, each chapter is self-contained, and may be read in the order you wish. After all, this is *your* journey. It may be interesting for you to note which chapters interest you the most. Follow your instinct, and have fun with it.

The themed chapters contain posts from Champion's Blog, which was the precursor to this book. "Broadcast Your Inner Champion" aligns the posts by theme. At the beginning of each chapter is an introduction which defines the theme and underscores why it's included in the book. I also share intimate memories of specific blogs and why I wrote them. I don't just write about these themes because I've done research and intellectualized their importance. I write about them because I've lived them. To me, it's funny how God works. How can I help anyone live a better life unless I shine my own light? Yet how can I shine my own light without going through serious life issues and challenges?

This book ends with the Epilogue. In it, you will be challenged to collapse all of your thoughts about the themes of this book into one answer to the original question: "Who are you?" Having answered that question, prayerfully in a refreshing and exciting way, you'll be ready to explore what "Broadcast Your Inner Champion" means to you. What does it look like when you do it? And who benefits?

A WORD ABOUT THE BLOGS

You'll notice that the blogs are written in different literary styles. Some are written as prose, while others are written with poetic license. As someone who writes poetry, I've found that my written pieces tell me how to write them. I hear the rhythm of the poem in my head before I write anything down. Given the creative nature of poetry, I often find that I must bend grammatical rules so that the poem comes out as it wants. Sometimes I have to suspend the rules altogether. I honestly can't say why this is so, but as an artist I always listen to my instinct.

When I started Champion's Blog, I noticed that my tendency was to write blog posts in much the same way. In fact, a few of the posts are poems of mine. The best way I can think to describe why I wrote the blogs as I did is this: sometimes when I make grammatical corrections to either my poems or blogs, the results don't *feel* right. The message/intent/feeling gets lost in the grammar. For instance, a piano player may play notes exactly as they're written down, and he plays them perfectly in the technical sense, but the music doesn't illicit the feeling intended. Another piano player may play the same piece, but hold one note a tad longer, or another note a tad softer…and the feelings engendered in the listener become powerful and meaningful.

This book, therefore, is designed so that you read it in much the same way you would a book of poetry. Within each chapter, the blogs will relate to one another by theme, but each will take you on its own separate journey of remembrance, and will prayerfully illicit their own particular feelings/thoughts within you.

WHAT TO DO

I've discovered that my journey to self-remembrance is not just about me. Many have impacted who I am and my self-awareness impacts the lives of many. In this light, I ask you to do the following throughout your journey through this book:

- As you read the blogs: *think!* How do you feel about what's written?
- *Talk* to friends and family about what you've read. Bounce ideas back and forth and continuously shape them through your conversations.
- *Discover* how and why you think the way you do.
- *Be aware* of the impact of others on you, and your impact on them.

I pray that your journey of introspection, connection and impact is as enlightening and powerful as mine has been for me. And may it bring you peace, love, joy and understanding that not only improves your life, but the lives of those around you.

I'll see you at The Epilogue.

Chapter 1

Self-Awareness

"I am no bird; and no net ensnares me: I am a free human being with an independent will." — Charlotte Brontë, Jane Eyre

"But you can't get away from yourself. You can't decide not to see yourself anymore. You can't decide to turn off the noise in your head." — Jay Asher, Thirteen Reasons Why

"Everything that irritates us about others can lead us to an understanding of ourselves." — C.G. Jung

Author's Notes:

According to Wikipedia, self-awareness is the capacity for introspection and the ability to reconcile oneself as an individual separate from the environment and other individuals. That's quite a mouthful. After reading that, I spent some time mulling over the intricacies of what self-awareness entails. What I got from the definition is that self-awareness begins with examining what makes us tick and why. As human beings we all feel compelled to find out who we are, where we come from, and why we're here. It's a feeling. A yearning. A desire so powerful that adults who were adopted as children will spend their entire lives looking for their birth parents, even if they experienced happy childhoods.

For me, self-awareness is explored in the answer to the question: "Who am I?" As I mentioned in the Prologue, this question is exceedingly complex, and has proven difficult to answer for most. I am convinced that the answer to the question is so important that one cannot become successful in life until the question is answered. How can I set goals for my life, know how to treat others, know what to expect from others in their treatment of me, know my relationship with God, understand my responsibility to my family, friends and community, or do anything positive in a sustainable way unless I truly understand and can articulate who I am?

If I am truly more than the name I am called, then how do I find out who I am? For me, the answer was simple: through my elders. My grandparents made a point of sitting me on their laps when I was a child and told me story after story about who they were as people, their experiences, the challenges they overcame, and even how they met. (Grandpa, of course, told a very different version of this story than Grandma did. His version included having to beat her off with a stick when she saw how handsome he was! Personally, I believe Grandma's version, but that's neither here nor there). Grandpa also made a point of telling me stories about his parents and grandparents, where our family name came from (it was shortened at Ellis Island), and what life was like for a young, Black male in Harlem in the 1920's. I'm still haunted by the image of him standing on a street corner, knowing he could not cross the street in one direction into one neighborhood, nor could he cross the street in another direction into a different neighborhood. The chains that kept him from crossing the street were not found on fences, but were imbedded in his mind by age-old social codes and long-understood repercussions for breaking such codes.

Of course, other family members and dear friends filled in the picture of who I am as well. Though I never met my father (he was killed in Vietnam when I was seven months old), Aunt Margaret, his sister, would regale me with stories about who he was as a man and a brother. My mom told me hilarious stories about their relationship. In particular, I loved the story about one time she and my dad "argued." She fussed and hissed, (if you know my mom, raise your hand), and my dad just sat there, growing quieter by the minute, and giving her a look that said "are you done?"

When Ma told me that story for the first time, I remember thinking about my dad's reaction: "Hey! That's what I would have done! I'm just like him!" It struck me like a bolt of lightning: they weren't just telling stories. They were telling me who I am. They were helping me answer the question in a way that fully explored the subtleties, the nuances and the fabric of what I do and why I do it. That experience was the foundation of my answer. Of course, there were many other contributors to my continuing understanding of my own self-awareness: my friends, my various communities, my experiences, my city of birth, and more.

The linchpin of my understanding is the image Grandpa painted for me: the little boy afraid to cross the street because of the color of his skin. I've often thought to myself: how can I possibly be afraid of the challenges I'm facing, when I've never come across something as humbling and dehumanizing as *that*? If he can overcome standing in his own neighborhood in fear, and all the other challenges of his life, and his blood flows through my veins, then I know I can overcome anything I'm going through.

And there it is. Though I grew up poor in The Bronx, I overcame. Although children I grew up with fell on every side of me to the dangers of the streets, I triumphed. I was not devoid of challenges. I faced them too. However, I faced them through the prism of a knowledge of self that gave me strength and power. I gained victories in life not so much through intelligence or anything I learned in school. As important as education has been in my life, my victories have come by remembering the stories of my past. That is why self-awareness is the first workshop in The Berlack Method, and the first chapter in this book. Facing life's challenges without self-awareness is like sailing the seven seas without a compass.

The Posts

The blog posts in this chapter were almost all the result of serious introspection. I wrote "Dust of the Earth," for instance, after reflecting on the pain of my past relationships. I also found myself going through a period of harsh isolation from friends and family. I made tremendous sacrifices when I founded The Berlack Method, and the weight of those sacrifices (financial stress and a tremendous battle between my faith and my fear) led to my pushing people away and diving into what I thought was a safe cocoon. While that was going on, I noticed something strange: whenever I became really tired and frustrated, someone would call me with an emergency. Either a family member had died, or a good friend was sick, someone had relationship problems, etc. I always got those calls at the exact moment I felt overwhelmed, and I learned two things from that revelation: one, we're all going through pains and disappointments in this life, and two, part of my purpose is helping people deal with their issues through the lessons garnered from my own pain. That particular epiphany confirmed my belief that knowledge of self includes understanding of purpose. This understanding put my issues in proper perspective: they were simply part of the process of growing into the role God had in store for me. "Dust…" was my attempt to capture that with words.

I wrote "Minority = Less Than" after many conversations concerning the term "minority" and what it means. My experience has taught me that self-perception and self-identification are powerful tools that can both empower and enslave someone. I remark in the post about the many times I've spoken to African-Americans and, whenever race came into play, perfectly sane, intelligent, confident men and women would drop their voices to a whisper when saying the phrase "White people." It would be funny if it wasn't such an indicator of the power of seeing oneself as a minority in a free society. In my humble opinion, seeing oneself as a minority represents the enslavement of the mind in full effect.

"The Antelope and The Lion" comes directly from my workshop on Attitude. It's an anecdote about the roles of antelope and lions during a hunt, and how each animal instinctively knows his/her role. We humans can learn a lot from them. I can't tell you how many times I've seen people who, due to title, personality, etc., played the antelope role in the relationship, stood with feet planted firmly roaring fiercely at the lion. And they kept roaring until they were figuratively eaten alive. Again, it would be funny except for the dire consequences one can face by not knowing one's role….

For Your Consideration

How do you answer the question: "Who are you?" Do you simply state your name, or do you have anything else to say? What were the experiences that helped to shape your answer? Who were the people that did the same? Is your answer a stagnant one, or does it change with time?

These are all questions I suggest you consider as you read this chapter. Talk to your elders and loved ones. Ask them to tell you their perspective of who you are. Contrast their answers with your own perception. Are they the same? How are they different? Then reconsider the question. If you've never done this before, prayerfully this is the beginning of a life-long process that will lead you to not only knowledge of self, but a true understanding of how you connect to others and why, your responsibility to them because of this connection, and the purpose that will lead you to positively impact your community.

I hope you enjoy reading this chapter as much as I enjoyed writing it. Here's to discernment, and I'll see you at the Epilogue.

NOISE

This is for anyone who's ever made a decision...and then heard nothing but *noise*.

I am here to tell you that if you ever stand firm in your convictions, if you ever make a decision based on your morals, standards and faith...then noise is exactly what you'll hear.

The bad part is that you'll hear the most noise from the people closest to you. They will have advice about every aspect of your decision. They'll tell you what you should do/should have done/couldn't do/can't do/shouldn't think about....

They'll ask you: how could you?/why did you?/how dare you?/why didn't you?/why wouldn't you?/shouldn't you have...?

And then they'll tell you: well I can't/I don't see how/that doesn't make sense/I don't understand/I'm not going to support that....

Noise. All of it.

Now...don't get me wrong. The people close to you whispering in your ear may have nothing but good intentions for you. And they may not. Those closest to you know your strengths and your weaknesses. They know what to whisper in your ear...depending on what they want from you.

So my advice is: make your decisions based on your faith and self-awareness. Then step back. Stop. Listen. Absorb what makes sense to you. And then completely and wholeheartedly discard the rest for what it is: noise. Let it go, and stand firm in your convictions. This is important because if you're not careful, listening to the noise can make you forget who you really are. At best, the people feeding you noise meant no harm. At worst, the point of all that noise was for you to forget who you are, or more precisely, for you to become what they perceive you to be.

Remember: people either see you or they don't. If they can see you...I mean *really* see you, then honor them and heed what they say, even if you ultimately don't agree with or implement their suggestions.

But if they stand close to you, yet still can't see who you are, then how is it possible for them to ever give you anything other than noise camouflaged as "good advice?"

Tune in to who you are, buttress yourself with faith, and tune out the noise. Your purpose awaits you.

DUST OF THE EARTH

We are born with our souls intact. Powerful. Knowledgeable. Self-aware.

Yet we enter this Earth through strife, pain and trauma, bloodied and sometimes bruised. And so the assault begins. No matter how loving our parents, how supportive our families, or how nurturing our communities, we cannot be protected from strife, pain and trauma that life presents us.

We get hurt.

As children we fall and scrape our skin, knock out our teeth and break our bones. We slowly (or quickly) pick up our battle scars. As adults, we weave tall tales around each one, sitting in front of fireplaces or laying under the covers, pointing to the "C" shaped scar on our elbows or the meandering decades-old line on our thighs, whose stitch marks remind us of old railroads tracks.

We get older and discover new aches and pains, almost daily at times. Joints that once bent gracefully now send sharp waves of pain if bent only slightly. Knuckles that once bent strong fingers into formidable fists now swell and ache in cold weather. Hearts once strong and steady now flutter. Legs that once sent us flying through the wind now falter.

People who should protect and nurture us strike us with their hands. The ones who know the most about us use words that stab unerringly at our hearts. And so we get scarred...inside and out.

We get disappointed.

Plans carried out with time, sweat and tears get destroyed in an instant. Loves get lost. Friends are forgotten. Eyes once filled with love and lust stare at us now with rage, or even worse, with indifference.

We seek love, comfort, family and friends. Yet for many of us, life rarely affords us all of these things at once.

Our tears of joy are always interspersed with tears of great sorrow and pain.

And so we change. Because hurt and disappointment are great movers and shakers in our world.

But there's the rub. Change we must. But *how* we change is up to us. Change for the positive...or change for the negative. We *will* change, because our movers and shakers are too powerful to resist. In this life, we all get covered in dust.

But if you want to shake off that dust...look in the mirror. Realize that coming clean again means that you've finally come to understand that you've spent your life trying to *remember* who you are, not discover who you are. Remember: the colors of dusk are always the same as the colors of dawn. You were who you were *before* the first dust of this Earth covered your soul.

Remember: you cannot be covered forever, because this Earth is too small for you. This dust shall cover you, but who were you before your first trauma?

Do you remember?

Steve Berlack

WHO AM I THAT I MAY TOUCH YOUR SOUL?

I am, by pure definition, a bastard. I am the son of an unwed mother in the South Bronx, whose father was killed in Vietnam when I was seven months old. I grew up in both hard-scrabble, burned-out neighborhoods, replete with gangs, and in peaceful areas with working-class folks just trying to make it from paycheck to paycheck. I am a Black Puerto Rican male in a society whose Fortune 500 company CEO's, politicians, media stars, comic book characters, Supreme Court Justices and history book heroes generally do not look like me. When I put on a cape and uniform and look in the mirror, I still don't look like Superman.

So who am I that I may touch your soul? Who am I that I dare to speak to the masses, providing positive impact on communities, families, school districts and corporate bottom lines? Who am I that I might connect those who call I Am by different names? Or who don't call Him at all? Who am I that I Am would stoop so low to look at me, to hear me when I call Him, or to give me visions of my purpose and my impact on this world?

<< It comes to me>>

Who was Moses? He trembled in fear when God called him to lead his people. He was so convinced of his inability to speak in public, and of his inability to do what God asked, that he begged I Am that his brother Aaron be there to help him. Did Moses know then about his start in life, drifting in that basket on the river? Was that the cause of his fear? Of his sense of unworthiness?

Who was Joseph that he should one day govern Egypt? The youngest son with eleven older brothers, who lived in an era when the order of birth meant everything? Though his father favored him, did that keep his brothers from throwing him in the cistern? Though God gave him dreams of his family bowing before him, did those dreams comfort him when he was sold into slavery by his own flesh and blood? Or when he spent those long, dreary nights in jail because of the false accusations of a spurned woman? How slowly did the bells toll for him in that dungeon? Did he know, on those dark nights, knowing where he came from, how he would one day save thousands from starvation?

Who was Elisha that he dared to ask Elijah for a double portion of his Spirit and God-gifted power? Who was he that he should see the wind, and the horses and chariots of fire? Or that he should take up Elijah's robe, and receive exactly what he asked for? And walk the Earth with kings trembling before him?

Who am I that I may touch your soul? That I may hear the stories of my family's past, and take pride? That I may know the history of my people, and take heart? That I may, by God's great gift, see the connections between us that others do not? That I may solidify and make real those connections and impact the world?

I am Steven. Crowned One. By definition a bastard, but by faith a royal being. Though I began this life on the streets of the South Bronx, I am part of The Body that stretches across space, time and understanding. I may touch your soul, as you may touch mine.

I am Steven. Who are you?

WHEN YOU DON'T KNOW WHO YOU ARE, OTHERS WILL TELL YOU

The story of 19-year-old University of South Carolina - Beaufort student Byron Thomas has gone viral. The reason why he's garnered so much attention (in print media, broadcast news and the internet) is because he is determined to hang a Confederate flag from his dorm room window. The kicker? He's *African-American*.

Read about it here. http://www.nydailynews.com/news/national/black-college-student-sparks-debate-hanging-confederate-flag-dorm-room-kind-weird-black-article-1.985611

So, how does an African-American man justify hanging a flag almost universally seen by people of his community (including his own parents) as a blatant symbol of racial oppression? To wit:

When I look at this flag, I don't see racism. I see respect, Southern pride. This flag was seen as a communication symbol....

Mr. Thomas is certainly correct in that the flag was a communication symbol. For Confederate soldiers, it symbolized the original idea prevalent during the formation of the United States: that each state was sovereign, in essence its own country, and that we were "united" only so far as we would provide protection against common enemies. How dare some "federal" government dictate who they could or could not own? Their flag communicated the idea of states' rights, under whose umbrella the racism that justified owning slaves (including the rape, torture and murder that kept them in line) flourished.

After all, without the idea of racial superiority, how could they truly justify their treatment of Black slaves? And without states' rights, how could they justify their ability to exist among states whose popular morals would not allow for such behavior?

Most of the media outlets place the First Amendment at the center of the controversy. I disagree. Mr. Thomas absolutely has the right to hang the Confederate flag in his dorm room. This is, after all, America.

The real issue is Mr. Thomas' self-awareness. When I read that he saw the flag as a symbol of Southern pride, I thought about where I'd heard that before. It struck me as ironic when I remembered. I'd heard that while watching film clips of KKK rallies. And while watching interviews of modern-day White Supremacists.

See, if you don't know who you are, others will tell you. Given that Mr. Thomas is just 19, I wonder how much he knows about himself. If he is like 9 out of 10 people I've encountered, I'd wager that if I asked him "who are you?" he would state his name and have little else to say. Without knowing what else to say in response to that question, it would be no wonder that he would incorporate what *others* have to say about who he is and what the confederate flag should mean to him.

The only equivalent to Mr. Thomas' view I could draw is a scenario in which a German Jewish student hung a Nazi flag in his dorm room window and claimed that he saw in the flag a symbol of German ingenuity and defiance in the face of the economic chaos brought on by the victors in WWI. Anyone who knows history would point out to that student the torture and suffering of his people under that flag. The only way one could focus simply on the logistical merits of raising up the *Third Reich* under such circumstances would be to totally ignore what happened as a result of its existence.

That's why I believe the Jewish community has rallied so fervently behind the cry: "Never forget!" It's not so much to hang onto the pain of the past as it is to follow the advice of Shakespeare as voiced by Polonius in Hamlet:

This above all: to thine own self be true,

And it must follow, as the night the day,

Thou canst not then be false to any man.

Farewell, my blessing season this in thee!

You cannot be true to yourself, Mr. Thomas, unless you know who you are. You have every right to hang that flag. The question is: who do you see when you look in the mirror?

NONE SO BLIND

"Who are you?"

What seems to be, on its surface, a simple question, is in reality stunningly complex. The more one thinks about the question, the more one truly understands its meaning, and the more one understands the information it tries to bring out of the respondent, the more time one has to take to truly answer it. The question seems simple only because we think of it in simple terms.

To wit: the vast majority of my audiences answer the question in my workshops by simply stating their names. They then sit silently...waiting for my response. I let the moment marinate, and stand silently with them for a while. Then, as if the thought just struck me, I would push back with: "But what does your name mean?" And there's the rub. Whether I asked the question in a staff training workshop, or a male youth training session, or in my classroom in an urban school system, the audience invariably flubbed its way through mumbled answers I could barely hear before finally shrugging their shoulders and sheepishly admitting: "I don't know."

Every once in a while, someone would shout out with great pride: "My name means ...!" And all who answered in that way would beam at me with smiles from ear to ear, and go on to explain how they came to know the meaning of their names, and what it has meant to them to have that knowledge. And, more often than not, the rest of the audience would shrug their shoulders again, or give the "know-it-all nerd" that *look* (you know the one). But for just a few in the audience, I'd see that light begin to flicker in their eyes. The complexity of the question begins to dawn on them.

Sitting here reading this, you might find yourself asking: "So, what's the big deal? Who really goes about their day *thinking* about what their name means? Like knowing that pays any bills or gets someone a job!" And to that I have only one response:

There is none so blind as he who would not see.

I submit to you that the answer to the question "who are you?" is the single most important concept you will ever contemplate or articulate. The answer to that question, so often lip-serviced with "my name is..." is the answer that will not only pay your bills, and not only help you find a job, but will ultimately lead to something much greater: your purpose. I tell you here today that you can never answer "why am I here?" until you answer "who am I?"

Steven means "Crowned One." If I didn't know that, then how could I allow it to imbue my spirit with the royalty within me that I am always conscious to present to others? If I didn't know that I am "Crowned One," then what compass could I use to orient myself on the vast landscape encompassed by my emotions, my mental state, my spirituality, my cultural roots, or my value system? Not knowing that I am "Crowned One" is like looking at a map of all the "Steves" I could be without a compass rose.

Because I know what my name means, I am able to define for myself who I am, how I respond to situations, how to treat people, and yes, even how I look for work and pay my bills. It defines how I make decisions. I am royalty. And I pay bills, look for work, talk to people and demand that they talk to me as though I am the living embodiment of my name. Because *I am*. And that's all part of my answer to the question. My name is only the beginning.

More importantly, there is a grave danger to you if you don't know how to answer the question with the complexity of answer it deserves. If you cannot define who you are, then others will define you *for* you. For instance, if you're an African-American, you may be defined by others as an "N-word." Even worse, those who look like you may define you as the same thing, and tell you some garbage like: "well, *we* spell it with an 'a,' so that's different!" Okay, go tell that to Malcolm X. Explain to Dr. King how the "a" makes everything different. Go tell it to Nat Turner. Or Ida B. Wells. Or Frederick Douglass.

"There are none so blind...."

And the same holds true no matter your race, gender, creed or cultural background.

So...

Who are you?

I ask it again. And I sit here at my keyboard, waiting for your answer.

MINORITY = LESS THAN

One of the themes I often address in my workshops is the fact that perception is a powerful influence on self-identity and self-worth. In other words, how we see ourselves impacts our attitudes and our "realities." For instance, how many times have you turned on a news report about a brutal small-town murder, and heard: "Those sorts of things don't happen *here*." Or, how many times have you turned on a news report about a family on welfare, and the family shown was "minority," even though the typical welfare recipient in America was a young, White female? (How many of you knew that)?

To be more specific, the term "majority" normally connotes not just superiority in numbers but in intelligence and value, while "minority" often connotes the opposite. Though we have made much progress over the decades, these connotations are still reinforced through media images, and/or lack of public images.

For instance, one need only research the changing imagery of people of color in Hollywood to see both our challenges and our progress. Or, one may look in on the U.S. Senate floor during any session to see an image lacking diversity, particularly for a body designed to represent all American states.

To combat this image issue, I've refrained from using the word "minority" to describe people for over a decade now. When I address my audiences, I typically challenge them to do the same. Why? Because identifying oneself as majority or minority, is simply a matter of perspective. Are we just Americans, or part of the larger global family?

I thought about this when I read a report on The National Policy Institute's website entitled *"Global White Population to Plummet to Single Digit—Black Population to Double."* The report, rather shockingly, predicts that the world's White population will fall to 9.76% by 2060. By contrast, the world's Black population will increase to 25.38% by the same year.

See the article here. http://thenationalpolicyinstitute.org/?=404;http://www.thenationalpolicyinstitute.org:80/2008/04/18/global-white-population-to-plummet-to-single-digitblack-population-to-double/&reqp=1&reqr=

The report is fascinating given the demographic trending alone. But there's much more to this story. I point out these numbers to insist to all who read this that there is no such thing as "majority" or "minority" any more. In a world getting smaller by the minute through technological advances in communication and trade, we can no longer, with any real accuracy, assign such arbitrary designations as those that have guided us throughout our country's history.

Before the internet age, people who saw themselves as "minorities" often did so at the risk of seeing themselves as "less than" in every way. And, unfortunately, there were those of the "majority" who saw themselves as superior in all ways. If you don't believe me, sit idly by and listen to "minorities" speaking to each other. Tell me if you don't, at one point or another, hear them, while speaking in a normal tone, all of a sudden bring their voices to a whisper when they say: "white people." As if they're afraid of being heard. They become timid and afraid as they speak those two words, as the shadow of a country's violent past flashes across their faces. I tell you that that shadow is not just a reflection of our violent past, but it is a reflection of our own self-perceptions. Minority = Less Than.

In 1914, the word "minority" wasn't even used to describe people of color. In 2014, the term, like our country's violent past, is slowly fading away. In 2060, it will have lost its meaning altogether, unless somebody else embraces it.

I say good riddance: to the words, to their connotations, and to the shadows of a violent past that gave them meaning.

THE ASHFORD & SIMPSON EFFECT

Like many R&B fans the world over, I was shocked and saddened to hear of the passing of Nicholas Ashford. After reading an article about it, I reminisced about the soulful and inspiring music written, sung and produced by Mr. Ashford and his beautiful wife Valerie Simpson. I spoke to family and friends about him, and everyone shared pleasant memories of where they were when they first heard tunes like "Solid" and "Ain't Nothing Like The Real Thing."

When I remembered that the duo also wrote "Ain't No Mountain High Enough," it struck me that their music has been deeply embedded not only in Hollywood and history, but in our memories and hearts. Given that, I was astounded to read that initially, the duo recorded songs as "Valerie and Nicholas," without much success. I was also surprised to learn that they originally sold their songs for 75 cents a piece. My first reaction to reading that was to think to myself: "What? They sold their songs for only 75 cents? Didn't people know that they would become THE Ashford & Simpson?" And then it hit me: they didn't.

As "Valerie and Nicholas," people placed value on them and on their songs based on what they perceived of their talents. Without hit records already in place, people simply couldn't see the "Ashford & Simpson" in them. I've never met them, but I would imagine that the only way they survived such a dog-eat-dog world as the music business was to know their own intrinsic value, to remember that they were doing what they were *purposed* to do, and that the value of their songs were never subject to the perceptions of others. By staying true to their values, they wrote the music that was right for them, and the value of the songs soon became obvious, and priceless.

They never let other's lack of knowledge about them determine the value of "Valerie and Nicholas." By remembering their true value, and by letting their God-given talents shine under a 75 cent light, they transformed Valerie and Nicholas into Ashford & Simpson. They transformed 75 cents into millions.

And guess what? All of us have value way beyond the ignorance of people's perceptions of us. And more importantly, all of us have value way beyond even our own ignorance of who we are or where we come from.

If you've never truly given thought to your value, *explore* it. If you're not completely clear about who you are or where you come from, *identify* it. And if those around you don't really know you or your value, *broadcast* it. It's up to you to transform the "Valerie and Nicholas" that everyone sees in you into the "Ashford & Simpson" that you truly are. You can turn 75 cent experiences into a million-dollar life.

GUEST ON MOBILE XTREME STREET TEAM RADIO SHOW: "SELF-HATE" PT.2

I had the honor on June 29, 2011 of being a guest on the Mobile Xtreme Street Team BlogTalk Radio show entitled: "Self-Hate" Pt. 2. MX Street Team's show airs each Wednesday from 9pm to 11pm. All of the guests on that particular show were greeted warmly and led into thought-provoking discussion by the show's hosts: Showtime, Shizz and Special K.

Check out the archived show here. http://www.blogtalkradio.com/mxstreetteam

For my part, I wanted to emphasize that self-hate is a complicated issue that impacts people from all walks of life. The causes of self-hate are as varied as the people who suffer from it. I thought it important for the audience to understand that self-hate is a symptom, and is never a problem in and of itself.

Having said that, I was given the opportunity to talk about The Berlack Method, the themes of my workshops, my background and experience, and what it means to "broadcast your inner champion." I stated on the show that the key to defeating self-hate is engendering self-awareness. It's difficult to hate yourself when you're fully aware of who you are and the obstacles overcome by those who've come before you.

Between the various guests, we discussed everything from The Berlack Method to The Psych Method, from Malcolm X and the impact of slavery to speaking the language of our inner consciousness. It was all excellent conversation and very informative.

I gave out TBM's contact information, including this website, and I look forward to hearing from MX Street Team's audience.

I want to take this opportunity to say thank you to Showtime, Shizz and Special K for all of the work they do with the MX Street Team, informing us about the issues that are important to us. And they're a hoot, too! They have the wonderful knack of speaking about important issues while supplying enough humor to keep the audience entertained. I look forward to being on the show again soon.

SELF-AWARENESS + RESPECT = PULL YOUR PANTS UP!

Matt Hinton, writing in the blog *Dr. Saturday* on yahoosports.com, reported on a seemingly random and senseless incident that spent some time in the news cycle. Deshon Marman, a safety for the University of New Mexico football team, was kicked off a plane at San Francisco International Airport for refusing to pull up his pants. According to an airline employee, Mr. Marman's pants:

"…were below his buttocks but above the knees, and that much of his boxer shorts were exposed."

The employee called the San Francisco police and reported that a man was exposing himself at the airport. The employee then asked Marman to pull up his pants, and he refused. Not only did he refuse the first time, but he reportedly refused a second time to pull his pants up once on the plane. After 15-20 minutes of "debate," Marman was arrested and charged with trespassing, battery and resisting arrest, and was held on $11,000 bail. Now, really Mr. Marman, was that worth it?

See Matt Hinton's entire post here. https://ca.sports.yahoo.com/ncaa/football/blog/dr_saturday/post/Grieving-New-Mexico-safety-hauled-off-plane-boo?urn=ncaaf-wp2673

Marshan's mother insisted that he was in an "emotionally raw state" after attending the funeral of a murdered childhood friend. That was one thing. She then added that he was targeted because of how he looks: a young Black man with dreads and baggy pants.

My initial reaction to reading his mother's comments was to (with some degree of humor I might add) remember a skit done by a Black comedian on the Dave Chapelle Show in which he claimed that he was being discriminated against in New York by cabbies who kept passing him by and refusing to accept him as a passenger. The comedian then informed the audience that he had video proof of this. I fell on the floor when the video showed the comedian walking the streets in broad daylight completely naked as he attempted to hail cabs. The video became even funnier when the comedian proclaimed over the video: "See? It's because I'm *Black*! This racism must end!"

Now...anyone who has read Champions' Blog knows how seriously I take the history and impact of racism in this country. I am clear that racism exists and continues to have an oppressively negative impact on all American communities. But let's all be clear: when you walk into an elevator in the middle of the 'hood, and stand amongst a pool of urine, know that White people didn't come from all over the city to pee in your elevator. When you walk along the streets in some of my old neighborhoods in the Bronx and see trash strewn everywhere, what you're seeing are the results of what we've done to our own communities.

Hinton, for his part, summed up his post thus:

"Personally, I feel a little dumber for having spent a portion of my morning on (this story), and for actually feeling compelled to offer this parting advice, applicable to any situation you can possibly encounter in life: When in doubt, always pull your pants up."

To which I say: hear, hear!! At some point, we have to look ourselves in the mirror. I find it hard to believe that Mr. Marman always wore his pants at the proper waist size and with a belt neatly fastened about him, then, because he was distraught over his friend, suddenly decided to let his pants hang off his...posterior. Instead of going into a diatribe about the historical context that explains why men wear their pants that way (please look that up for yourselves if you don't already know), I'll say this: *men don't dress with their drawers out for all to see!*

How do I know this? Simple: my grandfather (the predominant male figure in my life), always left the house either in a suit and tie, complete with fedora, or with a collared shirt and slacks with dress shoes. Always. I am self-aware because I've seen how a Berlack man dresses first-hand. I saw the pride and respect that was given to him from others in the street, based on how he presented himself. I've seen for myself how people responded to me when I wore my U.S. Army dress uniform around my old neighborhood while I was on leave. People who once saw me as "that kid," suddenly addressed me as "sir" and shook my hand as I walked by. I was taught that a man dresses with pride and dignity, and I can feel that pride in my own daughters' eyes when they see me in suit, tie and fedora. (Yes, the legacy lives on).

As for Mr. Marman, I say this: how you dress is a matter of how you want to be perceived. Do you want to be looked at as a man or as a boy? Whether or not you cover your attitude with "I don't care how others perceive me," know that how you present yourself has *impact*. The choice, and therefore the power, is always yours.

Black Sheep said it best: "you can get with this, or you can get with that."

THE ANTELOPE & THE LION

When I was young, I was fascinated by a show called "Wild Kingdom." It highlighted a different species each show, and demonstrated how they survived in the wild. I was entranced by the beauty of the animals, and by how unusual they were to my world in The Bronx. Though I just saw it as entertainment, and though I didn't get it at the time, I was learning distinct life lessons from each show. It's amazing how, where and from whom one can gain knowledge that lasts a lifetime.

In particular, I remember a show about lions. They are beautiful creatures to say the least, savage as much as graceful. They are also masters of teamwork. The females hunt in packs (that sounds like a whole new post), and know how to place themselves in perfect position to help each other once one of them decides to strike. They even know how to "play the wind" to their advantage, staying downwind of their quarry so as not to alert their sense of smell. Sure enough, once all are in place, one of them pounces, followed by the rest, and what occurs next is a mad rush of graceful athleticism, high drama and sometimes, a disturbingly bloody conclusion....

It wasn't until years later, and after some life lessons of my own, that a flashback of that show brought to the surface some fundamental knowledge I had unwittingly buried years before. I never paid attention to it as a child, but as an adult, I realized that the antelope always reacted the same way: they ran. Think back. If you've ever seen footage of this, or if you've ever been privileged enough to see it live, have you ever seen antelope, at the moment of the attack, stand their ground and roar at the lion??

Ever?

They always run. They know exactly who they are, and they know exactly who's chasing them. They have, as we would say: "no shame in their game." They don't allow pride to get in the way of their survival. A buck never decides that he wants to impress the does with his bravery, "roaring" off at the mouth and demonstrating to the lions that "he ain't no punk." The antelope never wonder why everyone else is running. They don't try to "figure it all out" first before taking action. They don't take time to ask for advice. They run. And they stick together in the herd precisely because they know that the "bad @$$" that always wants to do things on his own, and who always has his own agenda, and who never "needs anyone," has a nickname: TARGET.

I mean, can we learn a lot from the antelope, or what? How many of us "roar at the lion," knowing that we have nothing for the claws and teeth coming at us? How many of us have cussed out our bosses, then tried to explain to the kids why they couldn't have steak that night? How many of us thought we had razor-sharp claws ourselves, only to pull out some hooves when the stuff hit the fan? And didn't we try to play it off? "Shoooot, I didn't care about that (insert situation here: job, relationship, friendship, promotion, etc.) anyway!"

Amazing. Antelope don't have claws that can rip another animal apart. Their teeth don't threaten anyone. But they sure know how to survive. The antelope always run from the lions, demonstrating that, at least part of the time, they're a lot smarter than us.

19

On May 20, 1966, PFC Gilliam Moore, A Company, 1st of the 503rd, 173rd Airborne Brigade, attached to the 101st Airborne Division, was killed in action in the jungles of Vietnam. He was 19 years old.

You can find out more about him, including medals earned, by clicking here. http://www.virtualwall.org/dm/MooreGx01a.htm

He was "on point" and on patrol with his unit on what would be his fateful day. After hitting an ambush, PFC Moore was shot and hit with shrapnel from a grenade. His left arm, his strong arm, was torn off. He gave the last that he could give for his country that day, but not before whispering a message to his buddy who rushed to his side....

Forty-five years later, to the day, his son writes this Champions' Blog post in his memory and honor. It strikes me that he has been gone over twice as long as he was alive. Nineteen years old, with a 7-month-old son back home in the States he had never met. I sit here today, typing on a blog on my website, to be read by people on the internet; concepts unheard of on 5/20/66. As I type, I try to imagine what went through his mind in those final moments. Was it worth it? Did he understand fully what he was fighting for? Did he agree? Was he scared? Determined? At peace?

I think about what he sacrificed at 19. When I was that age, I was a sophomore in college. Drinking (legal at the time), partying, having fun, and even studying every once in a while. To this day, I've never faced anything like bullets, shrapnel, or the pure chaos I've read that war is. The closest I've ever come to it was by reading his letters written while in-country. At 45 years old, I can only imagine how I would handle war. At 19, I couldn't even have imagined it. Let alone giving up my life at the hands of the enemy during a war that was less-than-fully supported by my countrymen at home.

His friend, who heard his final words, made it back to the States and fulfilled his promise to deliver my dad's message to my mom. As far as I know, she has shared that message with no-one, not even me. A final message, whispered across 45 years, still alive in my mother's mind and spirit. A man, forever young, still alive in his son, who reaches across the internet and implores you to remember the sacrifices of my dad and all who have given their last full measure of devotion to our flag and our country. A spirit, still alive in two granddaughters he couldn't have imagined on 5/20/66. They look at his picture on the wall, proud and in uniform, and notice how they, and their dad, look like Grandpa.

A grandfather at 19. Forever young. Rest In Peace.

And Dad, if you never heard it during those turbulent times of 1966, I whisper this message, back across those 45 years, from my spirit to yours: Job Well Done.

LITTLE BROTHER

Before Israel Sullivan was born, his father - my cousin - Dustin Sullivan gave me the honor of being his godfather. To say that I was humbled would be an understatement. What can I teach him? How can I have a positive impact on his life? As someone who teaches young men about discipline, attitude and self-awareness, I knew that I could do no less for my own godson. So I decided that my first interaction with him would be to tell him about who he is: as a male, as a person of color, and as an American. But how to do it?

The night I met him, I made a point of looking into his eyes, and as he looked back into mine - the words hit me. I could scarcely put him back in his parents' arms and get to pen and paper, so that I may capture what He told me to write. God is amazing that way. He used my new bond with Israel to bring forth these words. I gave them to his parents and I share them with you now so that you may in turn share it with the young man in your life - searching for knowledge of self. To God be the glory.

Little Brother

Sweet soul wrapped in ebony
Blessed in masculinity
Our ancestors speak to you through me
And give to thee this charge:
Walk this Earth in soulful pride
Our happiness in your heart resides
Our pain and pleasure pressed inside
The hold of a slaver's barge
Remind you of your destiny
Before the chains with lock and key
Stood stalwart men in line with kings
Skin sun-kissed ebony

Your Brothers are calling….

Black like people of the sun
Crimson like dawn-filled sky
Purple like robes
Wrapped 'round your heart
Blue like truth you can't deny
Brown like Earth beneath your feet
Are your Brothers who've never died

They whisper in your soul….

Charged: To thine own self be true....
For those who know you not
Will live in fear of you
They'll try to tell you who you are
And what destiny holds for you

But your Big Brothers remind you....

You have crossed the burning sands
You've built empires with your hands
Hearken unto your name: Israel
God's chosen people
Go forth and bless this land....
Sweet history gives its charge to thee:
Cherish thy mother
Protect thy sister
Honor thy father
And thy brother's keeper be

AN AMERICAN QUESTION

In the February 8, 2011 edition of the New York Daily News, Halle Berry's contentious split with former beau Gabriel Aubry is documented. More specifically, the article brings to light that one of the points of contention is whether their daughter Nahla is White or Black.

See the article here. http://www.nydailynews.com/entertainment/gossip/halle-berry-ebony-magazine-daughter-nahla-black-one-drop-theory-article-1.135415

Berry justifies her belief that Nahla is Black by saying: "I'm black and I'm her mother, and I believe in the one-drop theory." This "theory," of course, references the 19th and 20th century notion that if a person has "one drop" of "Negro" blood, then that person is Black by definition. Aubry, on the other hand, is cited in the article as identifying their daughter as White, even being incensed at any suggestions otherwise.

To be fair, Berry acknowledges that eventually it will be Nahla's decision to identify who she is. However, it saddens me that both parents seem to completely miss the point. Perhaps instead of using Nahla's race as a custodial football, they should be focused on Nahla. As a parent, I would suggest that instead of talking about what Nahla is, they might focus on the question of to Whom Nahla belongs.

In all of my travels, and in all of the conversations I've had with people from various religions and beliefs, from Orthodox to Agnostic, I've never come across someone who has the sense that God cares about what we look like, what color our skin is, or what race we belong to. Irrespective of what name we call God, or whether or not we even acknowledge Him, the actions we take towards even one person have ripple effects that impact multiple people in ways we may not understand. For instance, if Person A murders Person B, is Person B the only one that's affected? I say the answer is clearly "no." Anyone with a mother knows what I mean.

It occurs to me that by arguing over what race Nahla belongs to, as parents, both Berry and Aubry pull Nahla away from who she truly is. A human being, a child of God, with a rich family history and tradition on both sides. She is connected, as we all are, to the human family, part of one body.

And just as a side note: isn't it amazing that none of us actually say "I'm an American" unless we're on foreign soil? So I ask you the reader: who are YOU?

Chapter 2

Faith

"All who call on God in true faith, earnestly from the heart, will certainly be heard, and will receive what they have asked and desired." – Martin Luther

"A faith is a necessity to a man. Woe to him who believes in nothing." – Victor Hugo

"As your faith is strengthened you will find that there is no longer the need to have a sense of control, that things will flow as they will, and that you will flow with them, to your great delight and benefit." – Emmanuel Teney

Author's Notes:

According to www.dictionary.com, there are several definitions of "faith." Following are the first three:

1. confidence or trust in a person or thing: faith in another's ability.
2. belief that is not based on proof: He had faith that the hypothesis would be substantiated by fact.
3. belief in God or in the doctrines or teachings of religion: the firm faith of the Pilgrims.

On the surface, these definitions encompass very simple concepts. Yet we fall within a wide spectrum of ideas and perceptions of what faith is and what it means to have it. Some people are naturally trusting, and live under the mantra that they'll have faith in people until they're proven wrong. Others take a completely different tack, and refuse to have faith in anyone. They operate under the notion that they can only trust themselves and that anyone, even a close family member, is a potential enemy out to hurt them. So how did we go from simple definition concepts to such diverse and complicated understandings of faith?

I submit that the biggest challenge lies within definition number 2. In a material world, humans naturally seek proof of their ideas, surroundings and mindsets. Proof is the only way to know that something is real. Conversely, what is real is only something that can be proven. Many people believe that if you can't see, taste, touch, smell or hear it, then it can't truly exist. Given the technological explosion we've experienced in the past few decades, it makes sense that we've come to rely more and more on science. In that world, proof is the be-all, end-all of fact. Proof is what justifies our thinking. Proof is what justifies our world.

Faith, on the other hand, denies one the fundamental comfort of proof. That is precisely why faith is at the very center of the science-religion debate. That brings us to definition number 3. The concept of God complicates our perception of faith monumentally. Consider some of His names: Jehovah, Yahweh, I Am, Allah, God, Immanuel, Abba, Christ, Spirit, Vishnu…and the list goes on. Religions the world over provide a multitude of insights into the existence of God, some similar, some quite different. The major similarity in religions is that they require faith. They require a belief in His existence *without* proof. Things get very complicated however, when one considers that various religions require faith tied to distinct differences in perceptions of who He is and how He operates. Atheists and agnostics, on the other hand, to varying degrees, challenge the very notion of God, and agree on the point that God cannot be *proven*. And so, the world over, we continue to struggle with the idea of faith, particularly in terms of how we deal with each other. One need only consider the history of the Middle East to understand my point.

As for me, my faith is tied to very personal experiences. My faith in people is tied to the fact that I have been blessed with extraordinary family, friends and strangers who have taught, nurtured and otherwise assisted me in ways I could never repay. My faith in God is tied to very specific dreams which taught me who I am spiritually. The dreams also taught me that I don't have to figure out who God is or how to call Him. Nor did I have to build my relationship with Him. It already existed.

The point is, whatever faith we may hold is tied to personal experiences. And *that* makes it very difficult to wrap our minds around faith as a collective unit.

The reason that a chapter on faith is included in this book is because it is a notion inextricably tied to all the other chapters. For instance, I would argue that it's impossible to be fully self-aware without knowing where one stands regarding faith. Without knowing one's relationship to God and to others, how can one know oneself? Faith is also at the center of our attitudes. For instance, I can forgive others and work with them because I specifically asked God to forgive me. I would be a hypocrite if

I continue to ask Him to overlook my indiscretions while I lambast those whose indiscretions affect me. That brings me to the next point: how can we possibly understand our spiritual connection with and responsibility for one another without knowing where we stand within The Body? Faith informs us how to develop our youth, strengthens our cultural connections, and, with the right attitude, allows us to build strong, lasting personal and professional relationships. Without faith, the heart of the other chapter themes is cut away.

This was a very interesting chapter for me to write. As I created these posts, I was mired in my own battle between faith and fear. For instance, I wrote "Faith > Fear" right after deciding to quit my job as a public school administrator and to develop The Berlack Method full-time. I left the comfort of steady paychecks because I followed my belief that my purpose lies in sharing my gift of motivational speaking, and my experiences regarding self-awareness and spiritual connection. I truly believe that my blessings are meant to be passed along through my God-given ability to share these ideas in a powerful and thought-provoking way. As God continued to remove financial and relationship obstacles, I realized that my faith was the vehicle of my progress.

"The Devil and I Am (Lived)" was written as a direct result of a life-changing conversation I had with Dr. Diva Verdun. Like anyone, I sometimes struggle with self-doubt. I was, at the time of that conversation, anxious about whether or not I had made the right decision regarding stepping out on faith and starting The Berlack Method. At night, as I was trying to sleep, I kept hearing the whispers we sometimes hear: "Why did I do that? Shouldn't I have done *that* instead? How can I possibly make this work?" Dr. Verdun listened to my concerns, then pointed out the relationship between The Devil and Lived. (If you haven't noticed it already, look at the words closely again). Once I saw it, I decided that I would live in my purpose, and not be deterred by any Devil, however he may be defined. I wrote "The Devil…" the next day, and I haven't looked back since.

"We've Never Been Touched" was the result of a conversation I had with my oldest daughter, Victoria. She had a dream in which she found herself being chased by some spirit that meant her and her friends harm. She woke up from her dream screaming, and when I ran into her bedroom, she clung to me crying. After hearing about it, I asked her if she'd like to pray with me to rid the room of that spirit, so we did. The next day, she was still frightened, so we discussed it. This blog highlights the thoughts I shared with her.

As you reflect on these posts on faith, I challenge you to consider where you stand. Do you believe in the benevolence of others, or do you believe that trusting them can only bring you harm? Do you believe in God? What name do you call Him if you do? Do you tolerate the idea that others call Him by a different name, or is there room for *your* faith alone? Most importantly, are you where you want to be regarding faith? If so, can you improve your level of faith? If you're not where you want to be, how do you get there? And there's the rub, no? How to get there? Well, think about it….

G.R.O.W.

Sometimes, life just goes haywire. At the most unexpected moment. And at the worst possible time. You may be moving along just fine along your planned path in life. You may even be going through life's normal struggles. You know, when things happen in your life that you're not too comfortable with, but you understand the issue and why it's happening, and you make the corrections necessary to make it through.

But then, when you least expect it, the people closest to you, the ones who say they love you, your friends, your family, your co-workers, your boss, and that little old lady you see walking along the street every once in a while with her groceries, all turn on you in venomous rage. They curse at you, argue with you, or worse, talk about you to common "friends" after spending the morning smiling in your face. People who claim to know you but who couldn't say what your favorite color is whisper in other people's ears, giving them "advice" and turning a knife in your back with every word. Then they see you the next day and say "Hey *you!*" Grinning from ear to ear. And you think it's friendliness and warmth you see in their eyes.

And in the recesses of your mind, you think: "why is s/he *so* angry over that?" Or: "That made no sense *at all!*" Or: "Who the Hades is *s/he* to talk about me as if s/he knows me?" Your gut tells you something's wrong. That something's not right. That you're missing something. You feel it in your soul.

I'm here to tell you that nothing's wrong. Everything is all right. And if you're missing anything, it's that these people are acting this way because you're being "pushed." That "push" is what you're really feeling. That "push" from one part of your life to another. From one page to another. One chapter to another. One friend to another. One foe....

Though it may be painful, someone is telling you that it's time to move on. And I know who it is. He doesn't want you to be stagnant in life. You have a mission. You have a purpose. And just as clay cannot be molded without fire, you can't move on without some pain. Sometimes a lot of pain.

So how do you make it through? How do you survive the madness? The false confusion?

It's easier than you think.

Just remember to **G.R.O.W.**

God. Rules. Our. World.

Ashé. Amen.

Have you G.R.O.W.n today?

GOD'S AT EVERY TURN

Walking in faith is difficult.

For one thing, living a faithful life means sometimes making decisions that, from the perspective of others, seem very strange. For instance, as Executive Director of a job training program, I would never advise a client to give up a job and steady income to pursue one's purpose. Yet, as a born-again Christian, that is precisely what I did when I founded The Berlack Method. My faith tells me that my purpose is greater than my paycheck, because my gifts, which are tied to my purpose, aren't about me. They're about the people out there who have been desperate for help, and who have been waiting for me to take my leap of faith. As a dear friend once told me, because my gifts are not about me, fear is hypocritical. The Bible tells me that worrying about myself makes no sense, and that worrying is just a sign that I'm not conscious of God's power and benevolence.

Mathew 6:26 (NIV):*Look at the birds of the air; they do not sow or reap or store away in barns, and yet your heavenly Father feeds them. Are you not much more valuable than they?*

I leave it to God to determine who or what is most valuable, but I know this: if He will take care of the birds of the air, He will most certainly take care of me. He's just *like that.*

I've been advised that it also makes no sense to pray *and* worry. God's not done with me yet, so I'm still working on that. Growing. Learning. Sometimes, in the middle of the night, when it's quiet and dark in the house, my worries infringe upon my mind. I get restless, I toss and turn, and I sometimes have difficulty sleeping. Maybe you know what I'm talking about.

But then, I remember:

God's at every turn.

Every time I get to the point of restlessness, and sleeplessness, and sometimes, when I even get to despair, God sends an angel my way. When I worry about how to inspire others, someone comes along and inspires me. When I reach a dead end and my mind and emotions stall, someone takes me by the hand and negotiates a new path with me. Shows me the way. When I wonder about what to say, someone speaks to me and triggers a chain of thoughts in my mind that I know I didn't plant. Or someone shows me a picture that triggers a connection to a theme hidden in my sub-consciousness.

God's at every turn.

He uses us to speak to us. He's always there. Whispering in our souls. Showing us pictures that only make sense now that we've experienced something. And when you call out the Angels, and tell them who you see them to be, they deny it. Humbly. And that's your proof.

And so I vow that tonight when I hit my bed, I will rest easy. Even in the darkness and quietness. Because He'll be there. He always is. So even though what I do may look strange to some, I rest easy knowing that my faith is not based on their understanding. It's not even based on mine.

I don't understand. I just *know*. No matter where I turn, He'll be there.

I will rest easy tonight. Will you?

THE DEVIL & I AM (LIVED)

With special thanks to Dr. Diva Verdun.

I am that I am.

The Devil says that fear will rule me. **I Am** says I will be guided by faith.

The Devil: I will never make it. I was a fool to make the decisions that brought me here. **I Am:** I am *exactly* where I am supposed to be.

The Devil: My finances will ruin me. I will never have the means to live in my purpose. **I Am:** I am already my most precious commodity, and I already have all that I need. Any future needs are already anticipated, and have been covered.

The Devil: I am weak. I cannot stand against the obstacles in my way. **I Am:** My strength flows from I Am, and as long as I Am, who can stand against *me*?

The Devil: All is pointless. There is no sense in my moving forward, or following through with my mission, because no one will understand, or receive my message. **I Am:** I Am the fruit of I Am. I Am has planted the seeds, and as long as I am open to receive, my actions will bear fruit too plentiful for me to count.

The Devil: All is pain. All is wretched. All are deceitful. All are hurtful. All are lost. **I Am:** I Am Love. And all who are I Am are washed in Love. All who are part of the body are *found* in the body.

The Devil: I am isolated. I am confused. I am alone. **I Am:** I am We. I am part of the body. I need but open my mind to I Am to know who I Am. I am *aware*.

The Devil: My future is chaos. My future is dark. My future is unclear. **I Am:** I. Am. Already. Written.

The Devil: I am chained. I am constricted. I am linear. **I Am:** My awareness is my freedom. The more I am *aware* of I Am, the more expansive is my thinking. The more expansive my thinking, the more *aware* I Am. I am the complete circle. I am 360 degrees.

The Devil is The **Devil.** I Am is **Lived.**

I Am that I Am.

Who are you?

WHEN YOU'RE FACE DOWN, STAY FAITH UP

We all get to a point sometimes where we have it all figured out.

We work hard. We sacrifice. We struggle to provide for our families. We plan and we pray. Then we plan and we pray some more. Then we pray a little more before we revise our plan.

And how we do plan! Some of us of course are better at planning than others. We can have the next fifteen years all laid out, detail by tiny detail. "First I'll do this by the time I'm X years old, then I'll move on to this by the time I'm X+3 years old, then I'll...." We even come up with Plans B, C, D and E!

All the time waiting. And waiting. And waiting.... When will our plans bear fruit? When will our blessings come?

One of the best quotes I ever heard about planning came from Mike Tyson. (Knowledge comes from anywhere and everywhere).

"Everyone has a plan until they're hit in the mouth."

That's exactly what happens. If life can do anything, it can hit us in the mouth. With authority. And power. If you've ever seen a boxer do the "I'm about to hit the canvas but I don't want to" dance, then you know what you look like when life catches you on the jaw. We do the dance because we're holding on to that plan and those prayers. "Hey, wait a minute, I *prayed* on it! Where's my blessing?" Then...BAM!! You hit the canvas. Ready or not.

So here's some advice. Even when you're face down, stay *faith up*. Because your faith is your prayer's engine. It's your faith, not your plans, that will get you off the canvas. So when your plans have gone awry (who hasn't been there?), *keep the faith*. Because we never hit the canvas unless there's something for us to learn before we get back up. And with faith, we *always* get back up.

Your blessings are still out there. You just didn't plan on this trip to the canvas. So while you're down there, remember Mr. Tyson's quote. And remember what it takes to get back up and receive those blessings.

Stay FAITH UP my friends.

WE'VE NEVER BEEN TOUCHED

Sometimes, we have *that dream*. The one in which we're being chased. And we're scared out of our minds. Running from the ghost, spirit, phantom, friend, enemy…that entity that we can see but can't make out. Hazy…misty…only visible out of the corners of our eyes. It threatens us, harasses us, gnaws at us, strikes at us, hisses at us, *frightens* us….

The scenes change crazily and haphazardly. A moonlit park one moment, an old, familiar classroom from 20 years ago the next, a boat we've never seen before, but that is so clear we can give all the details of it whenever we awake. We get the perception that the demons that haunt us are everywhere. To the point that we can't make sense of it. "How…? Wait…when did I…how did it…?" At the end, the demon always closes in. We can *feel* it. We can *sense* it. We can *hear* it. It raises to strike, gnaws its teeth to bite, reaches out to….

And then we awaken. Heart racing, sweat drenching our clothes. We breathe so hard and so quickly it hurts, and so loudly it roars in our ears. Staring into darkness, frightened, trying to remember the images in the corners of our consciousness.

If we remember (and even if we don't), there are always symbols in our dreams. A key is not just a key. A buzzsaw on the side of a building represents something. A boat is more than just a boat. We're being told who we are. We're told about our purpose and about those who oppose it. We remember the anxiety, the fear, brought on by the spirit angered at our self-awareness, and then….

With faith we can remember: we've never been touched. Teeth were bared but never bit us. Swords were raised but never cut us. Voices were raised to a fever pitch but our ears never bled. We fell, but never landed. No matter how frightening the enemy is, no matter how intensely he bared and gnashed his teeth, no matter how scary the weapon raised against us, we're still here. Tried and triumphant. Covered and blessed.

So, tell me again why we're frightened?

TRIUMPH OF THE ROSES

As I opened my front door this morning to take my girls to school, I was hit by a pleasant surprise. The first roses of the year bloomed on the bush in front of my porch. There weren't many, just two. But their presence promised more to come. I couldn't help but smile as my oldest daughter walked out ahead of me, stooped and smelled the first rose of spring. Turning towards me, she beamed a bright smile. "Mmmm…" was all she needed to say. The roses in front are pink, and always call great attention to themselves and bask in everyone's remarks on their beauty.

Curious now, I walked around to the side of the house, and, sure enough, there was one rose blooming in the bush overlooking the sidewalk. This one was red, strong and proud. Beaming. At this point, I could hear my girls "oohing" and "aahhing" cheerfully. What a way to start a Monday morning….

Then it hit me. There's much we can learn from these roses. Every year brings the winter of their discontent. They are tramped upon by children and neighborhood animals, pulled out, (just in appreciation of their beauty, of course), snowed on and frozen out. For all their beauty, they are not defenseless, however, as anyone who's been pricked by their thorns can attest. And so the battle continues, until they finally give way to the prolonged cold snaps of winter. Disappeared, and, to the untrained eye, gone forever.

Until a day like this one. Not quite hot yet, but with just enough warmth to promise more. And that's all they need. They bloom. Slowly at first. Just two. And another around the bend. Then five more. Then twenty. Until the whole of the yard is bursting with color and phenomenal beauty. And the scent! Glorious! Undeniable. Until one can't come into the house without bathing in fragrance. Pink in front. Red and yellow along the side and back yard. And they trumpet their beauty, in all their senses and splendor, as triumphantly as the year before. And the year before that. And the decade before that. And so on…and so on….

How do they do that? I don't do anything special for the bushes. (I'd love to claim a green thumb, here, but…). I don't take care of them. I don't put down anything special for the bushes to feed on. And then it hits me again. They're already taken care of. (For those so inclined, insert God here).

Is it a miracle? Hhhmmm…. An image comes to mind. I always laugh when I see a flock of birds on my yard after a hard rain. Feeding. Squawking feverishly. Tramping about this way and that on the grass, near the bushes. And I realize as much as they're getting, they're giving back, too. It's amazing how God works, isn't it? We get our blessings from the craziest places, and in the most unexpected ways.

So, in honor of the annual triumph of the roses, I say: take your blessings where you find them. Worry not about the winter of your discontent. It too, shall pass. Soon, spring will come. Even before it's warm enough for your taste, you'll find yourself blooming. Don't worry about taking care of it. Your triumph is already done. So go ahead, trumpet your beauty, and bathe us in the fragrance of your success.

DOUBLE-DUTCH WITH GOD

I remember when I was a little boy in The Bronx, as I ran to play either football or softball with my boys I would pass this group of girls playing double-dutch. I would always catch them out of the corner of my eye, doing something that I thought was silly. As two girls swung a doubled-up rope, some girl would stand at the end/corner, making this weird back and forth motion, swaying with the rhythm of the rope, waiting to jump in. I remember that I always used to think: "Just jump in already! Pppsssttt!! *Girls....*"

I didn't get it. First of all, double-dutch wasn't a sport. I mean, it wasn't anything my boys or I played, so, what was the point? However, what was weird was that, from an athletic standpoint, I could see how difficult it must have been to actually time your jumping with two ropes. And I had to admit, I could appreciate the skill it took to make different hops, turn around, move back and forth within the ropes, etc. I never told anybody that, of course! But it was that incessant waiting in the beginning, that weird swaying, that for some reason just annoyed me. *Just jump in already!*

I just had a conversation with a good friend the other day that reminded me of the old neighborhood, and my thoughts watching those silly girls. "Don't any of them play football? Why do they exist, then?" (I was a slow bloomer, all right)? My friend was telling me about how he's made some recent changes in his life. He was a little worried about all of them, but he had placed his faith in God, and was wondering about when he should make moves, and when he should just let God do His work. He was praying about it, and waiting.

BAM! It hit me. We all play double-dutch with God. Swaying back and forth to the rhythm of our lives, watching…waiting. Do we wait a little longer, or do we jump? How many of you have those friends yelling in your ear: "Just jump already! Take control! This is your life!" Throwing your rhythm off, causing you to *think*, to doubt…. But there's something in you, that *feeling*, that tells you the timing's not right. That you need to do a little more being still (which is not the same as not moving)! You can sway, you can do a little positioning, but it's just not time to jump yet. You know it in your bones. And the more you practice being faithful, the more you acknowledge the need to sometimes *be still*, the clearer you can hear your inner voice: "not yet…."

In fact, as you learn to listen to that inner voice, the rhythm seems to slow, the spaces between the ropes get huge, dust, sticks, dirt, obstacles in the way get blown off, and then you hear it again: "jump!"

And, as life would have it, you repeatedly mess it up. You step on the ropes, get all tangled up, make a mess, then step out and start to sway again.... You friends and family (and your enemies): "jump!" Your inner voice: "you'll know when...." You make better and better-timed jumps as you move on. All of a sudden, you find yourself doing a 180 degree hop and facing the other side, keeping your rhythm as you move. You're improving!! "Ahh shoot!!" Are you going to do a flip next? That move you've always thought you could do? You *feel* it, don't you? The ropes don't even seem to be there anymore, do they?

And there you go. Skipping the double-dutch of your life. God both at the ropes, and within you. No wonder your timing gets better and better. With that combination, how can you ever truly mess up?

LET GO AND....

Every once in a while, I'm reminded that the plan of my life is not mine, and that whenever I put my ego ahead of my faith, I get a spiritual spanking from "Daddy."

I founded The Berlack Method, LLC, because I finally recognized that my ability to speak publicly and hold an audience is a gift from God. We are all gifted by Him in one way or another, and our gifts are inextricably tied to our purpose. After much prayer and a serious leap of faith (that'll be another post), I realized that my purpose is to spread the message that each of us must explore, connect to and broadcast our cultural and spiritual inner champion, which in turn allows us to understand our connections to one another.

I left my job "chasing paychecks" and developed my firm and my message, and took action, all the while having faith that God would remove all obstacles, and open all doors. He would provide. As Jesus reminded his disciples in Luke 12:29-32: "And don't be concerned about what to eat and what to drink. Don't worry about such things. These things dominate the thoughts of unbelievers all over the world, but your Father already knows your needs. Seek the Kingdom of god above all else, and He will give you everything you need."

However, like the "child" of God that I am, I often need reminders of lessons I've already learned. And He always provides those lessons! Ever since I took my leap of faith and started spreading the message that He placed in me, God has erased every fear I had. He has placed the right people in my life at exactly the right time. He has opened doors I didn't know were there, and He has moved mountains from my path with the assistance of my little mustard seed of faith. He has proven, over and over again, that if I just stay out of the way, I will complete my mission, to His glory.

Yesterday, I grew a little frustrated that people were not responding to my posts as I thought they would. I'm writing every day, reading, researching, praying, and finally pouring out the words on Champions' Blog. But I'm not seeing the fruits of my labor. So my ego got hurt. Like the rambunctious child of God I can be, I decided to take action on my own, and message people, get them to see the powerful words they were missing. With great intentions, I created a huge message on a social networking site with almost 100 people, imploring them to "be inspired!" But we all know what the road to hell is paved with.

Instead of causing a mass exodus of readers who would "see the light" and "be connected," people were furious that their message boxes were filled with "Reply All" messages from people they didn't know, and the whole thing became a huge brouhaha. Hurt feelings, people defending this or attacking that. I created a huge, unadulterated mess. All because of my ego. How humbling God's lessons can be!

The good news: many people stood up for me, debating the "naysayers" and imploring me to continue my work. They told me that I must continue being a positive and thought-provoking person. Instead of inspiring them,

I was the one humbled and inspired by the people I thought of as my audience. Dr. Diva Verdun, a great friend and one whom I've come to recognize that God uses often to speak to me, reminded me that this isn't about me, but about Spirit, and that I'm positively impacting more people than I could know. I must be patient, stick to the work, and let God handle the ripening of the fruit....

And so I begin again. At the beginning. With a renewal of faith and a determination to do the work that will bear a fruit pleasing to God's eye. I start with this post.

I'm letting go...

...and letting God.

Ashé.

Amen.

WELCOME

I want to take a moment to welcome everyone to my new cyber-home: www.steveberlack.org.

This website is a testament to the power of faith. I'm here to give testimony that if any of you reading this believe that you have a purpose and submit your life to fulfilling that purpose, God will bless you with tremendous opportunities and resources that you may not have dreamed of. This website is that blessing and opportunity for me. When I founded The Berlack Method, LLC, I had neither the expertise nor the resources to produce such an eye-catching and effective website. However, I held true to my faith. I was certain that if I continued to develop TBM, God would provide what I needed to progress. Through (God/happenstance - what would you call it?), I met Dr. Diva Verdun, who developed the site with her God-given talents.

Broadcast Your Inner Champion

My job now is to pass that blessing on to others through my work.

Having acknowledged God, I want to thank Dr. Verdun for all of her hard work, vision and determination to make this site a reality. You are the best Diva, and truly The Illuminator!

Now, as for the site. Please feel free to explore the many interactive features of this website. Here you'll find:

- Video clips of my life skills training workshop, the BET Tonight Shows I've hosted, a clip of my Disney talk show pilot, my appearance on 60 Minutes, community forums and more. Check back often!
- Photo galleries of various aspects of my life and events related to my work, complete with music. Just let the pics load, sit back, relax and enjoy!
- A floating tag cloud that interacts with you! Play with it as much as you like. I do! You can click on any tag to take you to the blogs corresponding to it.
- A scrolling Twitter feed of my musings there.
- Champions' Blog.
- A blog calendar.
- An events calendar with particular event information and event lists below it.
- A ticker tape of important announcements.
- A page peel that unveils a picture of me with elements of my logo that directs you to my booking page.
- And more!! Just explore and enjoy! I take this site with coffee, but maybe that's just me! :-)

Thank all of you for visiting, and taking some time out of your busy day to spend with Steve Berlack and The Berlack Method, LLC.

If this site proves to be a blessing to you, then you know what to do....

WHEN YOU'RE CLOSE TO YOUR DREAMS

Sometimes, the hardest place is be is close to your dreams. When everything you've worked for, sweated for, sacrificed for and dreamed about is right at your fingertips, but not quite within your grasp, it can be torture.

Maybe your issue is money. "If I just had $10,000, I could *do* this!" Maybe your issue is time. Or family commitments. Maybe you simply don't know *how* to get over the hump and achieve your dreams. Maybe you don't have the support you need.

Often, people are much closer to their dreams than they realize. They struggle with the challenges of life, like always, and then BAM!! What others would call a lucky break occurs, and someone's life is changed for the better. Though they may suffer, I submit to you that it is agony of a whole new level when you're *right there*…at the edge of your dreams…and you *know* you're there…yet the end of the journey is still unknown. You still might fail.

And so maybe your issue is patience. The ability to hold on just one more day until that breakthrough. The ability to stay strong when your bills are bigger than your bank account. When the naysayers are at their loudest… whispering in your ear. They whisper so loud that you feel your eardrums will burst. Yet they're slick enough that no-one else hears them but you.

I may or may not be able to help you with the struggles of your life. The issues that hold you from your dreams. But I can tell you that the patience you need to HOLD ON…is born from faith. I am a witness that angels come your way when you least expect it. That you will find people you love and barely know alike standing by your side at your darkest hour… lifting you when you fall. Walking you across the goal line that lay only inches from your feet, but that you never would have crossed without help.

Your issue may be anything…but the answer to all is faith. You will *make* it. You will survive. You will achieve.

While windows slam in your face, I tell you….God will open doors.

Someone said that in my ear, that I may whisper it in yours....

FAITH > FEAR

As I sit here typing this, I find myself in the middle of a decades-long battle. Faith vs. Fear. More specifically, which of the two will be the driving force in my life?

My faith tells me that my diamond (define that as you will - my "true" self, my soul, my essence, etc.) will shine for all to see. That in the end, I will live in my purpose and help vast numbers of people to live in theirs and experience healthier, happier lives than they did before my assistance. My fear tells me that the mud, dirt, ash and blood that life has heaped on my diamond will not only keep others from seeing its sparkle, but will keep me from seeing it as well. That the vision of my purposeful life I see in my mind's eye will not manifest in reality.

The details of this battle are irrelevant. I say this because I've found that almost all of us struggle with the battle of faith vs. fear. The details of our battles differ from person to person. But ultimately, we must choose to fight with the weapons of faith, or succumb to the demons of fear.

I choose to fight. This is not a physical struggle. This is a spiritual one. This is a mental one. And an emotional one. I claim right here and now that my faith is greater than my fear. My diamond will be seen. I *will* live in my purpose. The visions in my mind's eye today will be tomorrow's reality. I choose to fight. What do *you* choose to do?

Chapter 3

Attitude & Success

"We are what we pretend to be, so we must be careful about what we pretend to be." — Kurt Vonnegut

"I am a part of all that I have met." — Alfred Lord Tennyson

"Keep your thoughts positive because your thoughts become your words. Keep your words positive because your words become your behavior. Keep your behavior positive because your behavior becomes your habits. Keep your habits positive because your habits become your values. Keep your values positive because your values become your destiny." — Mahatma Gandhi

"Whether you think you can, or you think you can't--you're right." – Henry Ford

Author's Notes:

According to Wikipedia, the term attitude is defined thus:

- Attitude (psychology), a person's perspective toward a specified target and way of saying and doing things
- Propositional attitude, a relational mental state connecting a person to a proposition

The definition of attitude is quite straight-forward. One's attitude is aligned to how one views his/her situation, and determines both speech and actions. It's my experience that many people live day by day without a sustained consciousness about the impact of their attitudes on everyday life. If I ask my audience about their attitudes concerning specific subjects or events, most can articulate them well. However, they typically find it much more difficult to generally connect the impact their attitudes have had on their successes and failures in life as a whole. In workshop after workshop, I've found that many fail to make this connection because of their perception of the word itself.

What strikes me about the term "attitude" is that it has a nearly universal connotation of negativity. Whenever I ask an audience to define the word they almost always conjure images of finger-pointing and eye rolling. If not that, they think of attitude as the mental state one has when one is tired, angry, jealous, or has given up on a task. It is exactly that stereotype that my workshop on attitude is designed to negate.

This chapter is, therefore, designed to change the way the reader sees both the term and its impact. Not only is attitude healthy, it is, in the proper context and in appropriate dosage, absolutely necessary to success in life. Attitude is, in my opinion, the lynchpin to success. If one has ever heard a doctor explain to a family member that one's recovery from injury or sickness will depend on the "fight" he or she has within, then the impact of attitude becomes crystal clear. Both the Gandhi and Ford quotes at the beginning of this chapter speak to the fundamental and cascading impact that attitude has on one's success or failure.

Where Does Attitude Fit In?

This chapter falls by design after "Self-Awareness" and "Faith." The answers to the questions: "Who am I?" and "To whom do I belong?" form the foundation of one's attitude. In The Berlack Method, Attitude comes after Self-Awareness and Faith because there can be no thorough understanding of how one thinks or acts without first exploring who one is, both physically and spiritually. Having answered those questions, one can see that attitude can indeed be empowering. With self-awareness and faith, the challenges of life will be seen not as obstacles, but as opportunities. Painful experiences become learning tools. Hurtful family and friends become memories that serve as foils for our inner happiness. Mountains become footstools, and enemies become our servants.

Now *that* is attitude….

The Posts

"The Peak & The Precipice" provides the formula for attitude. I wrote it several years after my Fulbright trip to Peru, which included a stop at Machu Picchu. As you might imagine, I told stories of this trip many times over the years, and I always shared a funny tale about the bus ride up the mountain. The bus driver drove *way* too fast for my taste, and I was shocked to learn that the narrow, curvy roadway up and down the mountain was a two-way road. After seeing numerous buses and cars flash by our bus, and my life flash before my eyes, I was through with that trip up the mountain well before we got to the top. It wasn't until I wrote this piece, however, that I realized that that one little bus ride was a powerful metaphor for my life, my attitude, and the faith that engendered it. I pray the formula for life I discovered in "The Peak & The Precipice" proves as fruitful and enlightening for you as it has been for me.

"In The Ring" serves as a natural metaphor for attitude and life. My maternal grandfather was a prize fighter as a young man, and taught me the art of the sweet science as a child. My father was a Golden Gloves boxer before he enlisted in the Army and fought in Vietnam. I've lived my life conscious of the fact that fighting is in my blood. As I became more and more aware of my spiritual walk, I found myself, as I had been forewarned, in a tremendous spiritual battle. The prize was my purpose. My struggles waxed and waned, but inevitably I found myself wading through some very dark days. As those days piled on, I began to realize that my opponent couldn't win, but could only make me think that I would lose. It was while I was in the midst of this realization that I wrote "In The Ring." May it bring you the same peace it brought me.

Few people know that I also write poetry. I struggle with finding the time to do so, but periodically, as life strikes me, I am compelled to write poetry that captures where I am mentally and spiritually. "Be" is one of those poems. One day I simply decided that would be what I wanted to be. Nothing more, nothing less. When you read it, challenge yourself. What do you want to be today?

Your Attitude

As you read the chapter, consider where you are mentally, emotionally and spiritually regarding your attitude and its impact on your actions. Are you conscious of your philosophy on attitude? If so, how does it inform your decisions when confronted with life's challenges? How does your attitude impact how you deal with others, especially those you disagree with, or those you don't like?

Just as important, how is your attitude informed by your answers to the questions: "Who are you?" and "To whom do you belong?"

Think about it, and I'll see you at the Epilogue.

IN THE RING

I've learned a lot by being in the ring with Life.

My first lesson: Life is a world-class heavyweight champion. And Life hits HARD. He's been around a long time, and is no rookie. He's trained century after century, decade after decade, year after year…day after tireless day…and knows all the tricks. He can hit with the left or with the right with equal power. And he can feign and feint with the best of them.

If you're not careful, you can get knocked out quickly. I know because I'm in the ring.…

I've been caught with a vicious left hook to the jaw, and gone down in a heap. My head swirling. My heart pounding. My legs shot. And I've gotten back up. When I did, I was cautious about getting hit with a hard blow. I learned to keep my guard up; block the heavy blows. So I didn't see it coming when he feigned the left hook, evaded my block, and caught me square in the nose with an overhand right. Down I went…in a heap again. The referee's voice registering faintly in the back of my mind…6…7…8. Then I'm up again.

Wary now…my legs shaky…I back up. Life pursues me…confident now. He constantly stings my eyes with stiff left jabs…once…twice…thrice. I can't see then as he feigns the heavy blow, fakes the overhand right…and pummels me with thunderous body blows that take my breath away. But this time, I don't fall. I grab Life by the waist, pull him close…and hang on. He shrugs violently to get far enough away to throw the finishing blow. Desperately I hold on. Angry, Life tries to break free of my grip. He knows he's close to the knockout. But I am stubborn. And I am strong.

And as the referee separates us (after all, I can't hold on forever), I learn another lesson:

I can take a punch.

My jaw is strong. My will is unbreakable. My mind is resolute. And in my chest beats the heart of a champion.

So who else should I fight, if not another champion? A lesser opponent wouldn't provide the challenge I need to wear my belt with pride.

Exhausted, frustrated, and punched out...Life looks me in the eye. He sees it now. He's in for the fight of Life. And I see the realization light his eyes as surely as he sees the light in mine. We both learn this lesson together:

I can throw punches too.

Life's countenance changes drastically as, bloodied and bruised, I square up. My mind sharpens. My pain falls away. My heart beats stronger, louder, faster, like a champion, as I feel my immense power, everything in me, come up from my legs, turning my hips, my chest and my shoulder as I unleash....

MUSIC OF THE MORNING

My head, buried in the pillow
Has one ear turned upwards
Towards the window...

It's way too early...
My eyes are tired and heavy,
And are shut tightly against
The early rays streaming
Through the window;
Crashing against my slumber
That is guarded by the softness of my pillow,
And my will to sleep "just a little bit more."

I swear my pillow-top mattress is talking to me!
Pulling me softly, gently back to sleep...
But there's something in my way;

Steve Berlack

Something familiar, gentle and very old.
Something so gentle, so familiar and so old
That I ignored it.
But it will not be ignored.
Will not be denied;
Until I hear it, absorb it
Take it in and honor it
For what it is….

It's the music of the morning.
And slowly, reluctantly, I hear it.
It's in the tree just outside my window;
And it's answered in every corner of my hearing.
The birds are singing!
Urged on by the same sun that I was fighting.
While my pillowtop was urging me to sleep,
The sun was urging them to serenade me
And all else who would STOP to listen
And appreciate their beauty.

A chirp, a warble, a call.
And then three others. Then five others.
Then a dozen. Then twenty.
Chirps in response to chirps.
Warbles in response to warbles.
Call echoes call,
And all combinations in between.
A full-throated melody…
Crescendos of sharpness
Carried by soft undertones.
All intertwined into symphony.
And at the greatest level of my consciousness,
The song is just for me.
Who knew a chirp and a warble
Could do all that?

And, incredibly, if the one you love
Is lying with you, and opens up
And is willing to *listen*,
They'll sing for your loved one too.
My God, how beautiful!
No matter what troubles you
Have in this world...
No matter where life takes you;
No matter what corner of the globe
You lay your head in,
If you just *stop*, and *listen*...
You will be serenaded by God's sweet music;
The music of the morning;
And the only things that change
Are the calls of the song.

THE PEAK & THE PRECIPICE

Some years ago, I found myself sitting in a window side seat of a bus speeding up a steep mountainside road. We were heading towards the peaks of Machu Picchu. I was there as part of a Fulbright Scholarship group, studying Andean and Afro-Peruvian history and culture. We were in the middle of our five week stay, and, for most of us, this was the highlight of our trip.

As I rode along, several thoughts struck me. First: I couldn't help but reflect on the fact that I had come a long way from my childhood in a two bedroom apartment in the South Bronx. I'd often wondered: why was I experiencing such an incredible thing as this, while some of my friends back home could only dream of it? I thought about the choices they had made in their lives, and I in mine. I also thought about the strong family support I had. Many of my friends could not boast about that. "There but for the grace of God go I...."

I next noted that the road we were on was barely wide enough to fit two buses. And it was exceptionally curvy. What was worse, there was no barrier on the outer edge of the road. I dared not look downward outside the window, but as I looked straight to the side of the bus, I was flabbergasted to find that we were literally climbing so high on the mountain as to touch the clouds....

Then the bus lurched around a sharp curve, and instinctively, I dug my hands into the seat in front of me. We were going (in my estimation) way too fast for such a steep, curvy, unprotected road. Then a funny thought hit me. This reminded me of the dollar cab rides I once took in Barbados, the drivers going helter-skelter through tight, narrow roadways, honking their horns in their irritation and scaring me, a poor American passenger, half to death. Then I remembered that they drove no differently than the dollar cab drivers in Brooklyn. Ah...connection and familiarity. I couldn't help but laugh.

I was still laughing when I was startled out of my daydream by the honking of a bus on the other side of the road speeding past us, heading downhill at a speed that had to be scaring some other foreigner out of his wits. It passed us in a blur, and I was just about to cuss the driver when I noticed that my fingers, even with well-groomed fingernails, had dug small cuts into the fabric of the seat in front. "This is ridiculous," I thought. "I did not come here to die on some backwater, lonely...."

Then I did it. Without thinking, I made the mistake of looking out of the window...and down. I was astonished at what I saw. At an incalculable distance from my window sat the train that took us to the base of this mountain. It looked like a toy. Between the train and my window was a wooded precipice, almost sheer in its angle of descent. That took my breath away, until I looked even further down, and noticed that I could not see the side of the road reaching outward from the bus. All I could see was the bottom of our vehicle, and the grass of the steep drop below. It looked like we were floating over the edge, and I couldn't fathom how, at the speed we were travelling, we hadn't already plummeted to our deaths....

I find it odd now that the thought didn't occur to me until years later: my entire life has been like that bus ride up the mountain. I've spent my life climbing that mountain, negotiating the curves and pratfalls at speeds I'm almost never comfortable with. Going too slow can be dangerous, but going too fast can be terrifyingly worse.

And so I hold on. Sometimes painfully so. And I take the ride. When I look to see how close I am to the edge, I'm always astonished, and many times fearful. And I always seem to be much closer to the precipice than to the peak. Sometimes I'm so tired of being razor-close that I feel almost compelled to just go ahead and go over the edge. Just let go. In fact, I know some friends, both at home in the South Bronx and other places, that have made that jump. They're so terrified of facing the danger of the climb that they consistently sabotage it. Worse yet, they're terrified of what will happen when they finally reach the peak. Scared of their own success....

So as I sit here today thinking about that bus ride, I remember that often the difference between success and failure is as simple as succumbing to fear and the precipice, or clinging to faith and the promise of the peak.

An equation comes to mind. Faith + self-awareness = attitude. It's the attitude created by these elements that allows one to do anything, overcome any obstacles, ignore any hate, and reach any peak. It's attitude that makes you look away from the windows at your sides and forwards to the road ahead, no matter how curvy it may be.

I, like everyone else, have a choice to make on my journey. I can look to the precipice, or to the peak.

Though the former often beckons me, I choose the latter.

Which do you choose?

AFRICAN-AMERICANS: WHY DO WE HATE OURSELVES?

I am proud to announce that on Monday, February 6, 2012, I served for the first time as co-host of the L.A. Says Show on BlogTalkRadio. My co-hosts include the show's creator, Tameka "L.A. Say" Anderson and Juana Wooldridge. Our first topic for 2012 was a timely one given today's socio-economic and political climate: "African-Americans - Why Do I Hate Myself?"

Listen to the archived show here. http://www.blogtalkradio.com/lasayinc/2012/02/07/african-americans-why-do-i-hate-myself

The guest speaker for the show was Dr. Umar Johnson, whose article "Until Death Do Us Part: 8 Reasons For Marital Failure Amongst African Americans" contributed greatly to the conversation. Dr. Johnson spoke eloquently about the myriad issues impacting self-perception in the African American community. He really caught my attention when he mentioned that a significant issue to deal with is the *real* ADHD, or "Absence of Daddies from the Home Disorder." That got the comments rolling! The audience included both callers and chat room participants, all of whom added to the conversation and asked thought-provoking questions that drove the eye-opening discussion.

L.A. Says team member Poetic Flow then graced the end of the show with a signature poem to tie everything together.

Team members Damion Olivia and Denise Minor keep the show flowing, and future listeners will be treated to several show pieces, including segments entitled: Hoodwinked, Radio Theater, and Too Great To Hate, as well as continued poetry time to keep the mood moving!

It's not too late, click the archived show and…

Sound Off!

IS MORALITY OBSOLETE?

I read a disturbing article in the September 23, 2011 issue of The Week magazine. (Has Morality Became Obsolete, page 14 - via The New York

Times). In it, author David Brooks "sums up the moral philosophy of most young Americans" by highlighting the refrain:

If it feels right to me, then it is.

Indeed.

Brooks cites the book "Lost in Transition" by Christian Smith, with Kari Christoffersen and Hilary Davidson, which describes the morals of our youth as "just a matter of individual taste." Moreover, he notes that Americans in their late teens and early 20s do not understand why judgments should be made on issues such as cheating on tests and infidelity. Though their parents (and those even older), clearly see these things as "wrong," our youth see them as decisions guided only by individual choice, without any connection to general value systems. Worse, they seem to feel no obligation to society. According to Brooks, the best way to sum up the morals of our future leaders is:

I guess what makes something right is how I feel about it.

So I ask you: what does this mean for us in terms of how we deal with each other? Both as a parent and former educator, I can tell you that many of the youth I've dealt with do exactly what they feel like doing, and exactly when they feel like doing it. They have little to no regard for consequences, nor do they profess to care about the negative impact of their actions on others. As a teacher, if I had a dollar for every time a student told me "I don't care!" whenever I scolded him/her about his/her actions, I'd be in the Forbes 500.

Worse yet, our children are perpetrating violence against each other by methods and by degree in ways uncommon to our elders. Not only are they fighting each other in schoolyards, as I remember, but they're beating teachers and putting them in hospitals for "offenses" such as taking a student's MP3 player. Not only are they engaging in fisticuffs in the classroom, they're shooting each other in the streets over something as monumentally silly as a gang's proclaimed "turf." (Never mind that not one of the gang members actually owns any of the land). When a student spends his class time showing off the cellphone picture he took of a dead neighborhood kid with a bullet hole in his head and blood running from his nose and mouth (true story), we are witnessing a moral dilemma of unprecedented scale.

Meanwhile, politicians and school administrators are wasting precious time and money arguing over resources and playing the blame game. Is it the teachers' fault? Is it the unions'? Is the system broken? But for me, the answer is very simple. I've said it before, and I'll continue shouting it to the rooftops until the message is heard:

As a parent, my child's attitude and moral standing is MY responsibility. Period.

Would it be nice if this world were fair, and if all Americans truly had equal access to resources and privilege? Of course it would. Would this be a better world if we all competed on an equal playing field, with no special regard given to any particular race, gender, culture or sexual orientation? Without question. However, until that day comes, I pledge to my community that I, as a parent, will do all that I can to instill the morals, values and sense of spiritual connection espoused in The Berlack Method into the souls of my children. I will work until my last breath to ensure that they reflect those morals and values because they are a direct reflection of the truth I speak. How can I do that for my clients, and not for my own children?

What are *you* going to do?

BE (BECOME ENTIRELY)

BE Inspired

BE Courageous

BE Blessed

BE Positive

BE Forgiving

BE Humble

BE Courteous

BE Kind

BE Healed

BE Thoughtful

BE A Blessing To Others

BE AWARE

BE Conscious

BE Free

BE Connected

BE Considerate

BE Forthright

BE Respectful

BE Daring

BE True

BE The Person That God Created You To Be.

Sometimes, it's just that simple. What are *you* going to **BE** today?

Steve Berlack

HEART TRUMPS HEART

Every once in a while, we get to witness something greater than the spectacle itself. There's no telling when or if it will happen, so when it does, it is always special.

The spectacle I witnessed was the 2011 FIFA Women's World Cup. Needless to say, I was rooting for the American Women, ranked number 1 in the world. Match after match, the ladies demonstrated the heart, discipline, stamina, fierce competition and high drama that is sports in general, and international sports in particular.

But two of the U.S. matches were greater than all of that, and each one caught me completely off guard. They reminded me that sports is a mirror of the struggles we all go through in life, and that sometimes, even when only one is declared the winner, we all win.

The first match that struck me was the U.S. quarterfinal against Brazil. Anyone who follows soccer knows about the tradition of excellence in Brazil. Given our ranking, this match promised to be special, but little did I know it would turn out to be the greatest match of any sport I'd ever seen.

The U.S. went up 1-0 early, and although Brazil dominated play, the American women held on to their lead well into the second half. In the 69th minute, an American defender was given a red card (tossed out of the match) for fouling a Brazilian attacker in the penalty area. Brazil was awarded a penalty kick. For those that don't follow the game, penalty kicks are almost certain goals. The American goalie, Hope Solo (has there *ever* been a better name in sports?) defied the odds by blocking the kick. One of the referees, however, made a hugely controversial call by declaring that one of the Americans entered the penalty area early, and awarded Brazil a second penalty kick. (This is extremely rare). Brazil subsequently tied the match, and the American women were faced with the daunting task of playing the rest of the day down one player to a world powerhouse.

It took tremendous heart for the Americans to fight to a 1-1 tie at the end of regulation. And their heart was tested even more when Brazil went up 2-1 on a brilliant goal by star player Marta early in the first overtime period. The two sides continued with that score until extra time in the final period. With just about one minute left, the American women tied the match on an incredible cross-pitch pass that eluded Brazil's goalie and was headed into the net by forward Abby Wambach. It was the latest goal (in terms of game time) in Women's World Cup history. The U.S. went on to win on penalty kicks.

I mention the details of the match only to highlight what it took for our ladies to win: HEART. Talent is great to have. Ambition is even better. But neither of those attributes matter if they're not accompanied by the heart it takes to overcome the inevitable controversies that are thrown at you. Even when things seem unfair, and even when the obstacles seem insurmountable, only your heart will make you successful.

The second match that struck me? The final - U.S. vs. Japan. The Japanese players not only overcame the talent and physical dominance of the U.S. women (we were generally taller and stronger), they overcame the heartache and disaster of the earthquake and tsunami that devastated their country earlier this year. They fought for country in more than a symbolic way, and their heart took them to the top of the world in women's soccer.

We can learn a lot from these incredible women. This was a tournament I won't forget, because in sport, as in life, only heart can trump heart.

CHOOSE TO BE YOUNG

It occurs to me that youth is truly wasted on the young. I mean, they have no choice in the matter. They *are* young. Being young means (inexperience and immaturity aside), they have energy, verve, vigor, excitement, athletic ability (more or less) and a general physical "feel-goodedness" (yes, I know I made that up - I'm getting older dagnabit, and can't think as fast as I used to), that we who are getting older can't help but be jealous of. By the way, you have no idea how much it pained me to say "we" in that last sentence.

But I have to face it. All of a sudden, that physical "feel-goodedness" (I'm aware I said it again, thank you!), is starting to slip a little. Now, my knees do the popcorn song when I walk up stairs. They like to remind me of how I abused them for years with my football, baseball, soccer, rugby, softball and bicycling. During my youth, there was never a weekend (and very few weeknights) that didn't see me out on some field, courtyard, street or other relatively flat surface that allowed me to run free and feel the wind in my face (and hair, but that's another story). Now my knees carry me gently around the golf course, and all would be well, if only....

Being a humble man I will tell you that I'm 48 years old. And if anyone is or has been that age, you'll understand if I tell you that I've been putting some serious thought lately into trading my old bicycle in for a motorcycle, complete with tattered denim jacket that reads "Born To Be Wild" on the back. And I'm not ashamed to tell you that my poor, old bicycle has been standing in my basement for some years now. I can't believe it's really been that long since I've ridden. To give you a sense of what a loss that is, when I was a kid in The Bronx, I used to ride my bike with my oldest friend Tootie from the South Bronx near Yankee Stadium, down the length of Manhattan to the Brooklyn Bridge, then back up Manhattan to home again. And it was fun! We broke a sweat, sure, but it felt good! We couldn't wait until we'd ride again.

Fast forward to now. Let me tell you what else occurs to me: being grown is not as cool as I thought it would be! If you're an adult and you're reading this, help me out here. As I became "grown," I got too busy raising kids, worrying about work, worrying about bills, planning for the future, looking at those strange gray hairs in the mirror, trying to remember when I stopped wearing size 28 waist pants, and I stopped playing the sports that I loved - because I just didn't have the *time*. I'm "grown" now, so I must concern myself with grown things. And because I don't have the time, whenever I try to actually do something now, I don't have the energy. If I ride my bike from the front porch to the end of the block and back, I'm hacking, gasping for breath, pulling some muscle I was previously unaware of, sweating like I stole something, and gulping down ten glasses of water like I had camel in the family.

Broadcast Your Inner Champion

Let me tell you something. One of the good things about getting some years under my belt is that, unlike in my youth, things *do* occur to me! (From time to time, at least)! And what occurs to me at this moment is that this whole "getting old" thing is for the birds. Yes, I know that as a grown man, I have responsibilities that I must take care of. But, unlike in my youth, I have a *choice* to be young. Or not. I may have put away childish things, but I refuse to give up being young! My knee has popped one too many times, dagnabit. And I've said "Oww!" once too often because I did something simple like turn around fast.

So I'm telling you today, that this 48 year-old man is putting off his mid-life crisis until his 80th birthday. On that day, I'll buy my "BTBW" jacket, and prop Mrs. Berlack on the back of my newly-renovated 1946 Harley with her skimpy, polka-dot bikini (hey, this is *my* mid-life crisis, darnit)!

Until then, I choose to be young. I choose my physical shape - and I choose muscular and healthy. I choose to work out in the mornings before work. I choose to eat healthy and drink plenty of water. I choose to break out my trusty old Fuji, and use leg power over horse power. (If you listen closely, you may be able to hear a "hallelujah!" coming from my basement). I choose to run until I feel the wind on my immaculately shaved head. (That's not my fault! I blame it on Grandpa and his genes). And I choose to live with the energy, verve, vigor, excitement, athletic ability and physical "feel-goodedness" of my youth.

What do *you* choose to do?

THE POWER OF MUSIC ON ATTITUDE

For as long as I can remember, music has had the power to directly influence my mood. At first, I noticed that if I couldn't understand why I was feeling a certain way, there was often music in the background that I may not have been conscious of that matched what I was feeling perfectly. Once I discovered that, I began to set my mood by finding music that matched what I wanted to feel. As a child and young adult, that often meant finding the right beat, the right speed. As I grew older, however, I started to pay attention to the lyrics. Instead of just wanting the right beat, I wanted the singer to "talk to me" about where I wanted to go emotionally.

Many people are familiar with this phenomenon. Some are not conscious of it at all.

When I give presentations on attitude and self-awareness, I'm often astounded at the level of anger many of my young participants feel. In many cases, their anger is sprung forth from a fundamental lack of self-awareness, coupled with an array of legitimate and horrifying circumstances. However, when I talk about cultural and spiritual connection, the lack of awareness often reaches an entirely new level. The May 13, 2011 edition of *The Week* magazine highlights a study that suggests a reason why: lyrics found in today's music.

As noted in the aforementioned edition of *The Week*, Nathan DeWall, a University of Kentucky psychologist, conducted a study with several colleagues in which they analyzed the lyrics of Billboard Hot 100 songs from the past three decades. This is what they found:

'In the early '80's lyrics, love was easy and positive, and about two people,' study co-author Jean Twenge tells **The New York Times.** *'The recent songs are about what the individual wants, and how she or he has been disappointed or wronged.' The study found a marked increase in the prevalence of the words 'I' and 'me' in song lyrics, and fewer instances of 'we' and 'us.' It also registered a jump in angry lyrics about hating and killing, and a drop in songs containing positive words like 'love' or 'sweet.' The researchers suggest that rampant narcissism may be making it harder for people to connect with one another.*

Wow. Talk about a smoking gun. If our children and young adults are responding to music the same way that I did as at their age, then we really are in trouble. When I compare what I read about the study with what I know anecdotally about youth and their disconnection with others, I realize we've all got a lot of work to do. As a father of 13 and 8 year-old daughters who listen to the radio constantly, I'm aware that it's incumbent upon all of us to pay attention to what they're listening to, and to consistently talk to them about what they're hearing and what they think about it.

It's bad enough that they're listening to songs about hating and being wronged (and let's not even get started on the whole "B," "H" and "N" word thing), but if songs about "I" and "me" keep them from seeing how their anger and actions spill over onto others, then where are we going as a society?

I keep talking to my girls. Even when I don't understand, I try my best to listen. Even though they protest, I make sure to put my "oldies" (and hey, when did '80's music become "old?") on the radio so they can hear songs about love and positive struggle. And I keep facilitating workshops, trying to reach and teach as many as I can about who they are, to whom they belong, where they come from and where they're going.

What are you doing about this? What does your music say to those around you? Inquiring minds want to know....

WEEDS IN THE LAWN

I spent this morning mowing the lawn. I have a corner house with the little hill on the side. You know the type? I have to mow the front lawn, the hill on the side, the front and side sidewalk, and the back yard. I strongly dislike mowing! I don't know about you, but the sun *always* goes directly overhead whenever I mow the lawn. It could be 9a.m., but the sun will still burn HOT and BRIGHT at its apex the moment I pull the lawnmower from the basement. I guess the silver lining is that pushing a lawnmower up and down and along the hill always provides a great workout. When I'm done, I look like I just ran ten marathons. By the way, did I mention that I'm allergic to cut grass? So I have to wear this surgical mask that makes me look like some sort of crazed, sudorific grass-hacker. Just sad.

Beyond all that, the work is labor intensive and it's...well...it's boring. But, in the end, all of that is not what bothers me. It's those darn weeds. They're *everywhere*! They've skipped from the neighbor's yard, to my yard, to the house across the street. I'd swear sometimes the lawns are more weeds than grass. I've used weed-killer (PLEASE - that's another post)! But there they still are....

Now, I must have been really bored this morning, because, as I was cutting my weed-field, a thought occurred to me. I've tried weed-killer that promised to rid my lawn of the darned things, and I've cut these weeds six ways 'til Sunday. *Every* week. Yet here they are. And I remembered, it doesn't matter what anyone promises you, or how many times you "cut out" the weeds, you have to get at the root to get rid of them. You have to get to the SOURCE.

Then I thought: how many "weeds" do we all have in the lawns of our lives? (Don't get me started on how many types of weeds there are: attitudes, family, friends, co-workers, stereotypes, pre-dispositions, self-esteem issues, etc., etc.). How many times have people promised us the solutions, cut the weeds for us and told us how to cut out the weeds ourselves? How many times have we struggled up and down the hills of our lives, going sideways sometimes just to get some relief? Yet they're still there, popping up exactly where you just cut the daggone grass.

Then the final questions hit me. The root of the issue: why do I keep *attracting* these weeds to my lawn? What am I putting out there that these weeds are feeding on? Is the seed that I'm planting really just fertilizer? Instead of just blindly cutting across the grass, shouldn't I be focused on how *deeply* I should cut? Instead of just cutting, should I pull? Or not just cut and pull, but use another weapon in this fight? (For those who are so inclined, please insert God here). And by the way, does it matter if I clean up my lawn if my neighbor's is still full of weeds? Won't they still skip onto my grass, as is their nature?

Maybe it was just hot this morning and I was delirious. But I'm telling you I had one of those moments of clarity. An epiphany. The work of cutting and clearing my grass will never be over. And I can't just cut across. I must go deep. I must address the root: my behavior and my actions that attract what comes to me, before I can even begin cutting, pulling or getting out the weed-killer. Then, once my lawn is clear, it's in my interest to look after my neighbor's lawn too. And s/he must look after his/hers, and so on, and so on. Or we'll simply continue to fight the same fight...day after day after day.

I'm willing to do what it takes. Are you?

AdjustMENt of Attitude = AdjustMENt of Altitude

It was my pleasure and honor to address the men of Morgan State University on Wednesday, April 6, 2011. The topic: AdjustMENt of Attitude = AdjustMENt of Altitude. Although most of us have heard variations of this theme before, the layout of the letters suggest the heart of the discussion. This was about and for MEN.

We closed the door to our "Man Cave" and talked about many issues important to men. In particular, I made a point to discuss where we were as men 100 years ago (This was in tribute to Kappa Alpha Psi. We're celebrating our centennial this year. The Brothers of the Alpha Iota sponsored this event). We then compared that to where we are as men today. Given all of the political, economic and technological progress of this past century, socially we discovered that we find ourselves in similar places, particularly in our own communities. We discussed the fact that many of us grew up in households without our fathers, and that the vast majority of our ladies are giving birth as single mothers. We discussed the fact that in some states, 50% of us are dropping out of high school. Given that President Barack Obama is in the White House, it became clear that political and economic progress does not in and of itself move us from boys to men.

We spent the rest of our time discussing how we *do* move from boys to men. The discussion was frank, real and honest, and I made a point of pushing these young men to consider the type of men they are today, and whether or not they've achieved the type of manhood they envision for themselves. To their tremendous credit, the young men were open to critique, praise and knowledge. They all participated eagerly and enthusiastically. I loved interacting with them.

I'd be remiss if I didn't note that a very brave young lady came in and sat herself amongst us in the man cave, taking diligent notes the whole time. I acknowledged her presence, which she handled gracefully, and we continued our discussion without hindrance. I would also point out that she clearly made an effort to not participate in the discussion, but to observe and take notes. If only we all did that from time to time....

We did not have the time to address all of the issues we could have, and wanted to, address. The most common feedback I got was that they wanted more time to talk, and that they'd like to do this more often.

I'm finding this to be true in all of my male discussions. Gentlemen are hungry for conversation with, understanding of and support from our own ranks. It's time for us to STAND UP for one another. It's time for us to be brave enough to be the leaders in our homes, our families and our communities. The young lady that kindly visited us was a reminder that we're all hungry for that.

Thank you to the Brothers of the Alpha Iota of Kappa Alpha Psi Fraternity, Inc. for sponsoring the event, Morgan State University for hosting it (as part of a month-long series of events celebrating men), and in particular, thank you to Mr. Kent Ballard, Ms. Toya Corbett and Ms. Towanda Barney of Morgan State University. There are countless others responsible for putting together such an important series of events, and there isn't room here to acknowledge all individually for their efforts. They are, however, greatly appreciated. Finally, thank you, thank you, thank you to the gentlemen who participated in the audience, and in turn enriched my life.

INNER CHAMPION > MISSING LEG

I read an intriguing article on thepostgame.com about Arizona State wrestler Anthony Robles. He won the Division I NCAA national championship in the 125lb. weight class. In and of itself, there's nothing remarkable about that. Someone wins every year. Until you consider that Mr. Robles, a senior, was born without a right leg.

See article and incredible video here. http://www.thepostgame.com/blog/good-sports/201103/one-legged-wrestler-wins-ncaa-title

Now if *that's* not broadcasting your inner champion, I don't know what is. This story is a reminder that no matter the obstacle, no matter the circumstance, there's a champion inside each of us. People will see that champion, or they will not, largely depending on whether or not we're willing to broadcast it. It was one thing for Mr. Robles to believe that he was a champion, it was another thing altogether for him to stand tried and true on the champion's podium, crutches under his arms.

His missing leg meant that he not only wrestled on the mat, but he undoubtedly wrestled his whole life off the mat, facing doubt inside and out. He assuredly wrestled with those who said there was "no way." If anyone asked him who's been his greatest opponent, I don't know that I would be surprised if he said that it was not defending champ Matt McDonough of Iowa, whom he defeated for the title, but himself. For he must have conquered long ago the inner doubt that we're all too familiar with. His Inner Champion became the National Champion of the NCAA.

So, what doubt are you wrestling with? Who are your "naysayers?" Is it you? Do you know where your inner champion is? If you don't, then remember Anthony Robles. And search again. If you do, then you know what to do. Broadcast your inner champion!

WE ALL COME IN CRYING

All of us come into this world crying. We're pushed, pulled, traumatized and finally...spanked. We all respond in the same way. Without knowing how to verbalize the "This is some BS!" feeling we have...we simply cry. And wait to see what happens next. And the bad news is...the whole event isn't even our choice.

The question is: how will you go out? What are you going to do with this precious gift of life? More bad news: while you're in this world, you will be pushed, pulled, traumatized and yes...even spanked. So what are you going to do about it? What will you be remembered for? What will be your legacy? What will you leave for those still here? Now that you can verbalize the "this is some BS!" feeling we all have felt, is that how you'll spend your life? Or will you DO something to have positive impact on those around you?

What will people say at your funeral? As you transition from this world to the next phase of life...will those you leave behind be crying? As you did when you entered this world? Or will they rejoice that they've had the honor of knowing you?

Here's the good news: The answers to these questions are all your choice. YOU decide through your thoughts and deeds how these questions are answered.

From now until that fateful day the ball is in your court. What are you going to do?

Chapter 4

Spiritual Connection & Responsibility

"Make your own Bible. Select and collect all the words and sentences that in all your readings have been to you like the blast of a trumpet." — Ralph Waldo Emerson

"Knock, And He'll open the door; Vanish, And He'll make you shine like the sun; Fall, And He'll raise you to the heavens; Become nothing, And He'll turn you into everything." — Rumi

"The moment God is figured out with nice neat lines and definitions, we are no longer dealing with God." — Rob Bell

Author's Notes

According to Wikipedia, the term spirituality "lacks a definitive definition, although social scientists have defined spirituality as the search for 'the sacred,' where 'the sacred' is broadly defined as that which is set apart from the ordinary and worthy of veneration. The use of the term 'spirituality' has changed throughout the ages. In modern times spirituality is often separated from religion, and connotes a blend of humanistic psychology with mystical and esoteric traditions and eastern religions aimed at personal well-being and personal development."

When I read that, of particular note to me is the idea that spirituality is typically separated from religion. One may not espouse a particular religion while still recognizing one's spiritual existence. Spirituality and religion are of course connected. It is for this reason that "Spiritual Connection and Responsibility" is included in this book, and is the next workshop in the suite of The Berlack Method. From my perspective, it is through the spirit that we are all connected. In fact, it can be argued that not only are we interconnected individuals, but we are part of One Body, one Spirit.

That brings me to the second part of the chapter title. If one indeed agrees that we share a spiritual connection, then what's the point? I would submit to you that if we are connected, then our awareness of this connection carries a price: responsibility. If you know that your words and actions not only have import, but impact, then are you not responsible for those words and actions? Are you not responsible for how your words and actions affect the lives of those around you? To stretch the point even further: are you not responsible for how your words and actions indirectly affect people you don't know, even in far off places you've never been?

Once one explores one's own faith, then understanding one's connection to others and accepting one's responsibility to them is the natural next step.

I explore this idea in my workshop that shares the title of this chapter. In a piece I call "The Tapestry," I ask the question: "Are you connected to a child born in India this morning?" The response always varies. Many simply cannot see connection to or responsibility for anyone besides themselves or those close to them. Throughout the workshop, I draw a visual depicting how the connection occurs.

Those that know me well know that my sense of purpose and connection to God comes through my dreams. If I have a question in my heart for Him, I'm often answered in the night while I'm sleeping. Those who are familiar with the story of Joseph and the dreams he shares with his family understand what I mean. However, I received a clear indication of our spiritual connection to one another by a dream that wasn't mine.

Not long after starting The Berlack Method, I was discussing an upcoming event with a colleague. Though I was excited, I was deeply fearful of the financial consequences of following God's direction and leaving my job (something I would never recommend) and pursuing my purpose full-time. After discussing the event, my first as President of The Berlack Method, I received a phone call. A dear friend informed me that she had just had a dream about me. She went on to explain that in her dream, I called her and, though she saw it was me calling, she didn't wish to pick up, so I left a message on her answering machine. I told her that I was eating Chinese food, and had before me three meals. From each meal, I had a fortune. Though none of the fortunes made sense individually, when I put them together, they formed a message from God. The message? "I have already planted the seed. All you have to do is nurture it, and your blessings will come soon." When my friend finished telling me this, I was floored. Who else but God would give someone a dream in which He brings me a message, which I pass to her in another message, knowing that she would in turn bear the responsibility to pass the message back to me? Tapestry indeed. Three words ran through my mind as I contemplated her call, and continue to do so today. Introspection. Connection. Impact. They are the perfect short definition of The Berlack Method.

The Blogs

"Student Driver" is a reflection of one of the most important and profound lessons I've learned: walking in our spiritual path means demonstrating the same love and patience for others that we ask of God. It also reminds me that each of our life experiences are connected, and that the lessons we learn from one event should transfer to another. I often miss this point, and "Student Driver" was written to keep me on the right "road."

I wrote "Bin Laden's Impact on The Tapestry" shortly after Bin Laden's death. I was sitting with my daughters as the raid on his compound and what led to it was being discussed on the news. It occurred to me that I had not discussed any of it with them. As a parent, I see it as my responsibility to teach them about their spiritual connection to and responsibility for others. As I shared with them my perspective on what happened, it dawned on me that one person alone can have a tremendous impact on the world. I also realized that the impact that my daughters have in the future may be informed by my own experiences if I use them as the teaching tools they're meant to be. I mean, isn't that why I had the experiences in the first place?

"Our Connection Is But A Whisper" was the direct result of a very public conversation I had with several members of a religious sect in Baltimore. Though their intent was to indoctrinate me to their particular beliefs, the manner in which our dialogue happened brought very clear and specific insight to me separate and apart from their intentions. I was overwhelmed by the power of the lesson I learned, and I pray the lesson is as profound for you.

The Questions

As always, I ask that you honestly consider the questions that may arise for you as you read this chapter. Are you connected spiritually to others? What is the extent of this connection, if any? Does death stop the connection? (Take a moment, marinate on that one). To whom are you responsible? What truths inform you of the extent of your responsibility?

Enjoy the blogs, and feel free to share them with others to get their thoughts on this. Discuss it with them. Do you all agree about your connections and/or responsibilities? Does anyone share an idea that impacts your stance, or vice versa? Think about it, and I'll see you at The Epilogue.

STUDENT DRIVERS

While on my way to a meeting this morning, I happened to fall in line behind a very slow-moving car on a narrow street. It took a moment, but I finally realized why the car was going so slowly. On the rear bumper was a large sign we've all seen before: STUDENT DRIVER. At first, admittedly, I grew impatient. I huffed and puffed, and I tapped my hand repeatedly on the steering wheel. I even had a rather one-sided conversation with STUDENT DRIVER in my head. (I won't repeat it here). Look, one of my growth areas is dealing with slow drivers, and I hate traffic jams. Hey, I'm a New Yorker, what can I tell you?

I briefly considered the old, tried and true New York car honk, but quickly decided against it. I mean, that *would* have been rude of me, right?

At that moment, as if nudged by God, I remembered when I was that student driver. I remembered the first time I drove on the highway, nervous and scared. I, too, rode my brake until it had my footprint permanently emblazoned on it. I of course don't remember this, but I'm sure someone behind me had the same reaction I had today. Impatient. Angry. S/he may have even honked that horn.

Nudged by God again, I realized that in every aspect of our lives, at some point we are all student drivers. Whether it's at our jobs, negotiating relationships, learning about ourselves, learning how to deal with others, breaking bad habits, understanding our spirituality and connection to others, etc. And we definitely have all been student drivers when it comes to understanding God. In fact, we are always student drivers when it comes to Him, aren't we? No matter what we may call Him, or how we praise Him, He is always the Master. He always knows the right road, and how fast or slow we should be moving. Yet there we are, scared, hesitant, and riding our brakes. And no matter how frustrating we may be to Him, He always, without fail, shows us patience and love.

Later today, while on a social media page, I had a very interesting conversation with a woman who, while disagreeing with me, cussed me and showed a level of anger that just seemed out of touch with our discussion. At first, I got angry as well. And for a hot second, I thought about cussing her back. I mean, I may be saved, but I wasn't *always* saved!

But then I remembered the student driver this morning.

That driver, as scared and as hesitant as he was, taught me to remember patience when dealing with others, if only because we all, at one time or another, need patience shown to us. In short, he reminded me how I should deal with my social media antagonist. I stayed calm, I stayed patient, and I responded to her with the respect and love I expect from all others. I never cussed, and I stayed true to the mantra of The Berlack Method: Broadcast Your Inner Champion.

I pray that Ms. Antagonist finds peace in her heart this evening. And I pray that I never forget that student driver.

WHAT IF GOD DISMISSED US THE WAY WE DISMISS EACH OTHER?

I just engaged in a fantastic discussion on one of my social networking sites. The question was posed about dating outside one's race. This is a complex and highly emotional topic, to be sure. The intensity of the debate as to whether or not we should date someone who does not look like us is a direct reflection of the wrongs we've perpetrated upon each other. These wrongs have led to hatred, racism, sexism and xenophobia that have divided and conquered us as a human family since time began.

As the debate raged on, I realized that we were making our points on two different levels. Those who were debating that we should not date outside our race were pointing to history and culture to buttress their remarks.

They pointed out the crime of slavery and persecution, in particular, as the reason behind their dismissal of other races as potential mates. Racism notwithstanding, I've heard it argued that differences in culture and world perspective are legitimate reasons to dismiss potential mates, if not to hate them altogether.

I, on the other hand, was debating on a spiritual level. I can remember, having experienced a "rebirth" as a Christian, walking around for days watching people as they passed me in the street, seeing them as souls, irrespective of flesh and blood. It was like looking at the world through new eyes…with new sight, and with a new light. As a Black American male, I listened to the debate about both history and *his* story, and completely understood the argument. As a Christian who has asked God for forgiveness, I found myself arguing: how can we dismiss a whole people because of the sins of some within their race?

What it comes down to for me is this: if I Am is I Am, then who are *we*? Are *we* just Black, or just White, or just Asian? And if it is true that we are all part of The Body, then what is there that connects us all more powerfully than Love? As the debate drew to a close (and I must say it was a thoroughly enjoyable one, as each one who engaged in it was respectful and articulate), I was hit by a stunning question. It was so profound for me that I had to pause before I typed it. **What if God dismissed us the same way we dismiss each other?**

I shudder to even think about it. What would our world be like then? What would we even look like? I don't know what side of the debate you fall on, but I do know that *I* would not want to be the one trying to look God in the eye to answer that question.

We are all connected and living under the grace of God's forgiveness. Dismiss and be dismissed. Love…and be Loved.

FORGIVENESS + HUMILITY = POWER

As I began my spiritual journey as a Christian, one of the most powerful moments of my life came when I asked God to forgive me for my sins, and I gave my life to Christ. It was such an overwhelming moment that I found myself prostrate and crying on my dining room floor, flooded with memories of my past that reminded me of what a great favor I was asking. That moment was powerful, but it was also liberating. I became free the moment I realized that if I were to honestly and truly ask for God's forgiveness, I must also forgive all who had "trespassed against me." It was right. It was balance. And it was the key to unlocking my future, for I was no longer tied to the anger, fear and distrust that I had come to live with as a result of my trespassers' actions.

That is my story and my light. As a Christian, I shine my light as I can, through my faith, my experience and my perspective. Yet mine is light in a world of brightness. I was thoroughly humbled to read a story of true forgiveness. Ameneh Bahrami, an Iranian woman, was permanently disfigured by the man who courted her. When Ms. Bahrami spurned his marriage proposal, Majid Movahedi threw acid in her face, blinding her. I cannot imagine what kind of torture that was for her.

See the article about it here. http://www.nydailynews.com/news/world/iranian-woman-ameneh-bahrami-saves-man-burned-face-acid-similar-fate-article-1.949509

In Iran, victims have the right to call for a literal manifestation of "an eye for an eye" justice. In her case, Ms. Bahrami was given the option of allowing a doctor to place drops of the same acid in her attacker's eye. In a moment of pure humility and forgiveness, Ms. Bahrami refused. Her reasoning provided a mantra that I will spend my life remembering:

It is best to pardon when you are in a position of power.

I was humbled to read this because I have not experienced such pain in my life. I realized that the more that acid ate into her flesh and disfigured her, the more pain and anguish it caused her, physically and emotionally, the more gracious her forgiveness became. And I was further humbled to be reminded that you don't have to be a Christian to show the God in you.

I shine my light, and Ms. Bahrami shines hers. With respect I submit to you that the forgiveness Ms. Bahrami displayed must come with a humility that would allow all of us to see past religion, race, gender, nationality, orientation or any other distinction. And I am humbled to witness Ms. Bahrami, through her ability to forgive, reclaim her power and her life from her attacker.

Thank you Ms. Bahrami for shining your light so brightly.

May peace and forgiveness bless all who read this. Amen. אָמֵן Ashé. آمين

PRECIOUS LIFE

One of the signature workshops of The Berlack Method personal development series is entitled Spiritual Connection and Responsibility. In it, I describe the intricate and infinitely complicated physical and spiritual connections that we all share. It is, if I do say so myself (but you don't have to take my word for it, check out the testimonials on this website!), a powerful presentation that causes one to think about the impact of each action one takes, how each action has repercussions often unseen and not understood, and about the responsibility we have for one another's lives.

This theme is evident in an HBO show called "Precious Life" that aired on May 5, 2011. The May 6, 2011 issue of *The Week* magazine gave this preview:

A Palestinian infant born with a severe immune deficiency appeared certain to die before adults around him forged and unlikely alliance. This documentary tells how people with every reason to hate one another - including an Israeli doctor, the child's fiercely anti-Israeli mother, and an anonymous Jewish donor whose son had been killed by Palestinians - set aside their differences when one boy's life hung in precarious balance. Powerful yet unsentimental, the film has garnered controversy and critical acclaim alike.

Powerful indeed. On the day that this child was born, could his mother have possibly known that a Jewish man she didn't know would have such a huge impact on her infant son's survival? At the moment the Jewish donor's son was killed, the subject of the documentary had not been born. Would the donor have been moved to help the young boy had his own son not died? Is it possible that his son was killed so that the other boy may live?

This is a stirring example of the oneness of mankind. In spite of religion, gender, culture or age, each of these people have direct and indirect impact on matters as fundamental as life and death. What if this young boy grows to become the man that finally brings peace to the Middle East, or invents the cure for cancer? Or simply becomes a great father to children who would never have been born had he not survived? How many lives would this young man impact then? And, just as important, would anyone bother to connect the actions of this anonymous Jewish man to these world-changing events? Or to the Palestinians that killed his son? Or to the mother who put aside her hatred to allow a stranger to help her son? Sadly, many would not.

It is not often that we think on this level. There are those who live their entire lives without giving thought to the universal impact they have on others. But the goal of The Tapestry presentation, and of "Precious Life," is to bring us there. To make us *aware*.

Know that you, too, have the power to change the world. Even if it is your indirect actions that make it happen. What you do with this power is up to you....

BIN LADEN'S IMPACT ON THE TAPESTRY

I asked my daughters this morning (they're 10 and 5 years old) if they knew who Osama Bin Laden was, or if they knew the significance of his death. They told me they did not. I had to think back: how much have I spoken to them about what's going on in this world? About the global impact of one man's actions?

My oldest was just a few months old when I found myself in Manhattan, about to attend class at City College of New York, when I walked into the crowded student center and saw the first tower fall. I didn't know it at the time, (nor would I until the list of victims' names appeared in the paper weeks later) but a very dear friend of mine was in that tower. I knew then that her daughter, about to start her freshman year in college that fall, was irreparably scarred. I realized even then, as the towers fell, that not only were thousands dying before my eyes, but an incalculable number of connected lives: family, loved ones, friends...were being changed forever. This moment dividing lives into "before" and "after" like a curtain between rooms. All this occurred through the thoughts and actions of one man... connecting to thousands of others.

I didn't know what to say to them, so I simply told my girls a quick version of the story of how Tori (my oldest) was in her crib at home when Daddy experienced a day in which he had to wait endless hours in Manhattan amidst the great confusion and disturbance of 9/11. I then told her how grateful I was to see her at the end of a historic day. I told Chrissy, my youngest daughter, how grateful I was that I no longer worked near nor was visiting the towers on that day, which meant that I could one day be her Daddy....

But as the hour approaches when I will pick them up from school today, it occurs to me that there is another story to tell. If one man can pull the threads of the tapestry of our lives with such devastating results, couldn't they also pull on the same tapestry to bring about incomprehensible good? Could I not teach them that they, with the grace of God, are the skeins through which the tapestry is weaved? That they have power? That because of that power they have the responsibility to *think* about how they pull the strings?

Though Osama Bin Laden may have thought of death and destruction as his mission, I submit to you that he is only another strand, connected though we may despise it, to all of us. It's up to us to use that connection, and twist it within the tapestry to create benevolence. We can do that by teaching our children that no matter their intentions, their actions have power. And their actions affect the lives of all of us, even if they don't understand how. Osama Bin Laden didn't have to know my friend to change her daughter's life forever. Just as my children don't have to know yours.

I will teach my girls to pull the strings of the tapestry for your children's benefit. What will you teach yours?

OUR CONNECTION IS BUT A WHISPER

I recently had the pleasure of interacting with members of a particular religious sect on the streets of Baltimore. They were resplendent in their traditional gear, and were presenting a powerful presence through their microphone and speakers. They were preaching the Word. I had not seen them in Baltimore before, but was familiar with them from my hometown of New York.

They were doing as I always remembered them doing, speaking loudly and eloquently trough the loudspeaker at the crowd passing by. They were articulate and intimidating speakers, in that their voices were loud enough and full of enough conviction that they hardly needed amplification. Their flowing robes replete with ancient symbols made them stand out completely from the people walking nearby, and somehow seemed to funnel their voices outward, making them even louder, and drew the attention of all.

They clearly knew the Word, and were reading from the Bible for all to hear. In the midst of this, one of the members and two young "officers" (as he called them), approached me. I greeted him in their ancient Middle Eastern language, and he returned the courtesy. With that, he asked me questions related to the people of the Middle East, their place in the Bible, and their connection to a very particular community here in America. I told him what I knew, but it became clear, as he continuously cut me off from speaking, that his aim was not to listen, but to discern which angles with which to convince me of what he had to say next.

He had one of his "officers" read from a clearly prepared text, and I had to stifle a laugh when I noted that the young man read in a loud, staccato voice that reminded me of DMX. Don't get me wrong, I love DMX, but the juxtaposition of that voice and the Word was just, for me at least… incongruous. He clearly was trained to read this way, yet given that we were standing next to each other, his voice sounded not just loud but forced and unnatural. I quickly realized that he wasn't reading to me, but was reading to get the attention of those around us. I then noticed that all within earshot were now watching us engage in our discourse.

I was struck by several thoughts at once. First, I realized that I had become part of grand theater. There was noble purpose attached to this theater: I was to be convinced that theirs was the answer and the true way to God. Second, I realized that the point of their discourse was that they were God's "chosen" people, and that I was connected to them by birthright. Third, I realized that I was being recruited to become a member of their sect. The leader made that clear when he invited me to come to their next training session. I was also struck by their great intelligence and obvious mastery of the Word. They clearly knew the Bible well.

I could easily see how, if someone were not clear about his/her own spiritual walk, one could be easily impressed by them, and inclined to follow their path. I don't wish to be disingenuous. Theirs is a noble cause: to bring people closer to God. However, their leader said one final thing that caught my attention. He said: 'I would really love for you to come to our training, because if you don't, it won't go well for you." Those words struck me like a lightning bolt, because it connected me to similar conversations I've had with members of other religious groups, with far different beliefs, who also warned me of my doom if I didn't obey their call. And I realized, through all those years, my own spiritual philosophy was born, and in that moment it came cascading around me, washing over me like rain. "I cannot help you shine your light by talking about your light. I can only help you shine your light by shining mine."

And with that, the whole point of our conversation came to me: our spiritual connection is not loud. It is not theater. It is neither staccato, nor braggadocious. It is neither colorful nor eye-catching. Indeed, it is but a whisper. It is fragile. It is so frail, that anything above a whisper threatens to break it. The symbols used to bring some closer to God can be used to exclude others. Our spiritual connection to one another is so delicate that it can disintegrate before our eyes upon our temples and within our tomes.

I truly thank the gentlemen that took the time to speak with me that day, for they are on a path to God. Though it was not their intention, they reminded me that we must protect this connection of ours, this fragile cord between us. We must whisper it with our actions, instead of shouting it with our words. For with each shout, each virulent wave of symbols, each hardened ear and stony heart, our chords but fall away. They helped me learn and shaped my continued path to God, though it may not have been in the fashion they desired. And isn't that its own lesson: that we impact people in ways we don't understand? Aren't we all getting humbled when we finally stand before Him?

I whisper this in your ear, that you may whisper it in the souls of others.

Amen. Ashé.

WHAT HAPPENS WHEN WE DIE?

What happens when we die? This is a question that man has asked from the beginning of time. The fact is, of course, that there is nothing we can prove about the afterlife. However, one need only peruse the internet, watch television, or know of someone who has had a near-death experience to get anecdotal evidence that there is life after death. As I think back upon the many stories I've heard about near-death experiences, several things stand out to me.

First and foremost, irrespective of a person's race, gender, culture, language, geographic location or religion, near-death experiences are almost all the same. They almost all contain clear, specific elements: a tunnel or funnel with a light at the end; a light or colors that we do not experience here; a connection to those who have died before us; a feeling of peace and/or of being "home," and an overwhelming sense that love surrounds us and is our foundation.

As I reflect on this, I find it difficult to explain how I feel. As I've previously mentioned, I started The Berlack Method out of a sense of purpose and mission, and I'm writing Broadcast Your Inner Champion as a reflection of that mission. Whenever I'm asked to describe what this book is about, three words pop into my head, as if they were placed there. The words I use to describe Broadcast Your Inner Champion are: introspection, connection, impact. I think about the stories I've heard about the afterlife and near-death experiences, and I realize that they confirm the messages I've received in my dreams. This book has the purpose to deliver the same message that those who've nearly died have received: we were who we were before the traumas of this life touched us. The stories confirm for me that our journey will bring us home as we remember who we truly are, spirits of love and light connected in ways we don't understand. They confirm for me that no matter what we call God in this lifetime, and even if we don't call Him at all, He is there with us as we journey home to ourselves, and we experience Him as Peace and Love.

The stories I've heard in which people see their deceased loved ones when they "cross over" remind me that we are connected to everyone, past, present and future, and that we only perceive our experiences as linear and time-bound here on Earth. I'm reminded that our connection to one another is rooted in Love and Peace, and it makes me feel embarrassed that I've ever wasted time arguing about politics, race, religion, who's right or wrong, etc. In the end, when we're all together again and feel ourselves connected to our source of Love, I have the sense that we'll all share a good laugh at what we didn't know as earthly beings. And we'll laugh again at how right we *thought* we were.

So what happens when we die? I have not had a near-death experience. I cannot tell you that I saw what's on the other side. But as I sit here typing this, I can tell you without a doubt that I can feel what happens when we cross over. I'm convinced that we do not spend this life discovering our identities, but we spend our lives remembering. I'm convinced that when we fully remember, we cross over and go home.

I suppose, however, that until that question is answered, the real question is: what happens when we live? Do we have to have a near-death experience to remember who we are? Do we have to see our old loved ones to know that we're connected? Do we have to travel a tunnel of light and come back to Earth to know that our connection brings responsibility? I say no. I pray that if this book does anything for you, dear reader, it brings you to the three words that echo in my mind: introspection, connection, impact. I pray that it inspires you in much the same way that near-death experiences have inspired those who've lived them.

Remember who you are. Know that you are connected to all and rooted in Peace and Love. Live your life as if you know what happens when you die, and that what happens is fantastic in a way that words can't describe. And before you go home again, take that Peace and Love inside you and give it to all around you. Even if you disagree about their politics, their views on sex or if they profess a different religion. Even if they don't look like you. Even if they call God by another name. Even if you say you loathe them. Give it, and give it abundantly. Because your Peace and Love will be replenished when you come back home. Prayerfully, I'll see you there, and take my fill of the same.

Chapter 5

Cultural Connection

"The first step - especially for young people with energy and drive and talent, but not money - the first step to controlling your world is to control your culture. To model and demonstrate the kind of world you demand to live in. To write the books. Make the music. Shoot the films. Paint the art."
— Chuck Palahniuk

"We seldom realize, for example that our most private thoughts and emotions are not actually our own. For we think in terms of languages and images which we did not invent, but which were given to us by our society." — Alan Wilson Watts

"I am pessimistic about the human race because it is too ingenious for its own good. Our approach to nature is to beat it into submission. We would stand a better chance of survival if we accommodated ourselves to this planet and viewed it appreciatively instead of skeptically and dictatorially." — E.B. White

Author's Notes:

According to Merriam-Webster Dictionary Online, culture is defined thus: 1) the beliefs, customs, arts, etc., of a particular society, group, place or time. 2) a particular society that has its own beliefs, ways of life, art, etc. My experience is that the term culture means different things to different people. Many people I talk to think of culture as whatever is "popular" or that which is generally shared and/or understood to be true. For instance, a majority of people in a particular geographic area may like a particular kind of music, so much so that the music binds them in shared memories, emotions and truths about what it means to them. Conversely, another group of people in another area may share the same bond over a very different type of music. These bonds may be powerful, which is a great thing, but the question remains: what happens when several cultures wind up in close proximity to one another (such as in America)? Too often, this cultural proximity leads to strife, misunderstanding, prejudice, hate and even violence. Therein lies the rub, and why "Cultural Connection" is a significant part of The Berlack Method.

I'd like to point out, first and foremost, that I don't just speak about culture and how it's defined, but I focus rather on the idea that all cultures have inherent connection. Importantly, these connections, at least in my experience, are almost invisible because people tend to focus on their differences. The point of the "Cultural Connection" workshop, and this chapter, is that by bucking the trend and focusing on our cultural similarities, we amp up the true power of culture to bind us and work in harmony with one another. Just as important, culture, once connected to others, becomes an inclusive and expansive bond, and is not limited by our own prejudices or vision.

This chapter is an especially personal one for me. I was fortunate as a child to have grandparents who were adamant about teaching me who I am by explaining our family's history. I immediately understood that when my grandparents told me about the day they met, or about their experiences and challenges overcome while growing up, they were really giving me clues to my own identity. The more they told me about our history, the more I came to understand my connections to everyone.

For example, if I were to ask you the reader to describe me, you would most likely agree with my workshop audiences that I'm an African-American male. However, when I tell you the family information that my grandparents told me, I'll ask you to re-evaluate who you see me to be. To wit: My father was Puerto Rican with the last name of Moore. His last name was Moore because his mother was adopted by an African-American family. So, now what am I? What if I was to share with you that my maternal great-great grandfather was a Prussian Jewish immigrant, who married an Apache woman upon arriving in the States? Now what am I? Throw in the fact that another of my great-great grandparents was a French immigrant and you might just throw up your hands and give up trying to classify me altogether. What if I was to also share that my roots to Africa go not through the United States but through Puerto Rico? Am I still African American?

There is, however, another point in my family history that speaks directly to the purpose of this chapter. When my great-great grandfather married, he was effectively ostracized, and our family split along racial/cultural lines. There are White Berlacks and Black Berlacks, and we have, over the years, had very limited contact with each other. Now, if our name was Smith, that would be one thing, but with such an uncommon name, is there any doubt that we're connected? Yet I have personally experienced interacting with a Berlack who refused to acknowledge any tie whatsoever.

The Blogs

I wrote "Our Common Language" in response to a magazine article I read that day. The article gave scientific proof to my anecdotal experience that we all share common roots that we ignore. This ignorance can lead us to behave towards one another in horrific ways. I couldn't help but feel a sense of justification while reading the article. I have spoken to audiences about our connections for years, and am always astounded at how consistently we ignore similarities in our language and other cultural elements. I remember thinking after reading the article: "We are one people! Get over it already."

"Under My Hoodie," as you may have guessed, was written in direct response to the Trayvon Martin case. Needless to say, that case struck a very personal and emotional chord with me. I saw myself in Trayvon, and I saw my grandfather as well. Grandpa told me stories about how he used to walk with a mirror in his hand when he travelled the South in his Army uniform during World War II. Black men in uniform had to be constantly on the alert, because they were automatic targets for lynching and torture. I found myself thinking: "how could anyone hate me or someone who looks like me? If they only knew me….." Upon completing that thought, I wrote this blog post to explain.

The Questions

As you read this chapter, consider: what do you know about your cultural and family roots? How does this knowledge impact how you interact with people with similar roots? How do you interact with people who are different? Are you willing to explore cultural similarities between you and those that don't look like or sound like you? If you recognize these similarities, does that change how you see yourself?

As I mentioned, this chapter is personal to me because of how far my roots spread, and because of how deeply my self-identity embeds in them. How far do you roots go? Ponder it, and I'll see you at the Epilogue.

Steve Berlack

UNDER MY HOODIE

Under my hoodie lies the mind of a man that has absorbed knowledge and self-awareness like a sponge.

I read texts and listened to instruction in school about who I am. I also learned about who my heroes are, and what my enemies look like. I learned that a man came to these shores and discovered this land, even though people were already here. I learned that I was to dismiss my common sense, and simply ignore that anomaly, and any like it. I listened to my elders, and learned something else entirely. I read on my own, and discovered that "truth" has more than one perspective. I discovered that no school can teach me who I am, but that I have to find that out for myself. I discovered that I am responsible for my own education; for feeding my own mind.

I carry that under my hoodie....

Under my hoodie beats the heart of a champion....

I am the product of a single-parent home in a depressed economic community. I've heard the naysayers as they glanced my way, shaking their heads and telling me I have no chance in this world. I listened as the Bursar at my University opened my files and told me about all the paperwork I was missing. When I responded that I had submitted the necessary papers, and wondered why she waited until the beginning of the Spring semester to call my attention to all of this, she shrugged her tired old shoulders and simply said: "That's y'all's problem. Y'all don't know how to take care of business." I remember sitting astounded as I wondered who "y'all" was. And then it dawned on me why she insisted I meet with her alone. I knew then precisely who she meant.

And so, a Master's degree, Fulbright Scholarship, Army service, teaching and public school administrative career, Malik Shabazz Human Rights Institute Scholarship, non-profit Executive Directorship, talk show pilot, nationally syndicated talk show hosting gig, motivational speaking business and various other accomplishments later, I think of that old Bursar, and, with fist clenched firmly, pound the heart pumping proudly under my hoodie.

Under my hoodie are raised the eyes of a man that can see.

I see the little boy who stood in front of the mirror, towel draped about his neck, and who, to his horror, realized he looked nothing like Superman. I see the woman who doesn't look like me that clinches her purse to her side as she steps onto the elevator I've been riding. I see the ads in the magazines. I see the television commercials. But I don't see me. What I do see is the face of the security guard who follows me through the large department store with furrowed brow and right hand at the ready.

I see an America that doesn't see me.

I see an America that refuses to look under my hoodie.

What do you see?

WHAT'S THE "AMERICAN" IN " -AMERICAN" MEAN? THE DASHED IDENTITY SYNDROME

At the time I attended Phillips Academy (Andover), there were students on campus from all fifty states and twenty eight foreign countries. At the City College of New York, I was just as likely to hear Spanish or Mandarin as I was to hear English on the yard. As a member of the U.S. Army, I engaged in daily work and play with people of every color, hue, gender, orientation, and linguistic/cultural background. As I engaged them throughout my life, I always did so as the African-American, Puerto Rican male from the South Bronx whose family roots ranged from Native America to France to Prussia and beyond.

As I continued to learn and grow from such an enriching circle of friends and family, I noticed that we all identified ourselves based on our roots beyond America. For instance, everyone would identify themselves as Italian-American, or African-American or Chinese-American. Given that I grew up this way, I found this to be quite normal. So much so that I never really considered what the "American" in all of those dashed identities meant.

However, something really interesting happened to me when I traveled outside of the United States. While I was in Geneva, if someone asked me what my nationality was, I would proudly identify myself without hesitation: "I'm American." It struck me like lightening the first time I said it. I felt no need to put a dash in my identity. No pressure. No need to explain. "American" said it all.

So what is it about being home that makes us all feel such pressure to dash our identities when we engage with one another? What makes us focus so much on the "Italian" or the "African" that the "American" loses its meaning? More importantly, we've become so divided in this country that the "American" has even lost its bonding affect among us.

Today, all it takes is a cursory glance along the racial and class divides of this nation to conclude that we are as fractured a culture as we've been since the Civil War.

What happened to the Americans that toiled together tirelessly in the rubble of the World Trade Center and Pentagon in the weeks after 9/11? From all accounts, none of them cared about the cultural roots or identity dashes of the people digging in rubble next to them. They were Americans. And that was all that needed to be said.

Yet today, we find ourselves turning on the news to find one crowd yelling "We are the 99%!" on one end of the divide, while on the other the crowds are yelling "We want our country back!" I don't know about you, but for me this all begs two questions: Just who are 'we?' And how do we give meaning to the "American" in " -American?"

What's your answer?

Broadcast Your Inner Champion

OUR PRESIDENT FINDS HIS APOSTROPHE

Even before the "Birther" movement, Americans were familiar with President Obama's Kenyan roots. It says a lot about how far we've come in this country that we elected a man whose middle name is Hussein and who is, by pure definition, African-American. What a lot of us aren't aware of, however, is that the President's great-great-great grandfather hailed from Moneygall, Ireland. This fact was duly noted when President Obama visited the Emerald Isle.

The President, by some accounts, "shook every hand in Moneygall," and his hoisting of a pint of Guinness at the local pub made headlines across the globe. Fintan O'Toole wrote in *The Irish Times*:

There are lots of people who look a bit like Barack Obama but are as much Irish-American as the obvious Micks…. 'Irish' is not a racial category.

O'Toole reminds me that we have much more in common than is immediately obvious. Who would look at President Obama and think "Irish?" Yet there he was, in a pub with his mates, connecting to long, lost roots that never disappear. It reminds me that there is a branch of the Berlack family that traces its roots directly to Prussia and Jewish culture, without the stops in Puerto Rico and Native American culture wherein my immediate roots run. Yet, we're all Berlacks. Connected. *Rooted*.

In New York, during the Puerto Rican Day parade, the saying goes: "Today, we are *all* Puerto Rican." In a real sense, in a rooted sense, President Obama reclaimed the O'Bama in him. May we all do the same.

OUR COMMON LANGUAGE

Anyone who has seen my workshops knows that the prevalent theme of The Berlack Method is the idea that we are all connected. That connection takes on many forms and manifests in many different ways, which provides a lot of material to talk about. One element that many of us overlook is language. Because there are so many languages worldwide, and because they differ so much from region to region, we often look at language as an indicator of the differences between us. A study conducted by University of Auckland psychologist Quentin Atkinson suggests otherwise.

The article "Is All Language Out Of Africa?" in the May 6, 2011 issue of The Week magazine (page 24), cites the Atkinson study, which theorizes that the world's 6,000 languages are all descended from a single ancestral tongue that developed between 50,000 to 100,000 years ago in southern Africa.

Atkinson tracks the movement of language by noting the descending number of phonemes, (basic vowel, consonant and tonal sounds) present in each language as one moves outward from Africa. This pattern indicates the presence of what's known as "the founder effect," which is the tendency of smaller groups to narrow the diversity of a larger population as they move away.

The science of that is fascinating to me, but that may just be a reflection of my nerd-like tendencies. More to the point, the Atkinson study provides further proof that it is our ignorance of who we are and where we come from that leads us to interact with each other based on perceived differences, leading to hate, jealousy, oppression and worse. No matter the cultural or linguistic differences between us, we all share the same roots.

It is my belief that knowledge of our common roots - our common language - is the awareness that we need to change how we do business with each other. Perhaps when we internalize how *similar* we actually are, we can change this world for the better.

Wake up people, and see our similarities! Am I speaking your language?

THE DIASPORA

I just read a very interesting essay entitled: "Why it is Necessary that all Afro-Descendants of Latin America, the Caribbean and North America

Know Each Other More." I found this essay on the Black in Latin America website.

See the full essay here. http://www.pbs.org/wnet/black-in-latin-america/essays/essay-why-it-is-necessary-that-all-afro-descendants-of-latin-america-the-caribbean-and-north-american-know-each-other-more/163/

The author, Tomás Fernández Robaina, is a researcher and professor of the National Library of Cuba. In his essay, he talks specifically about the struggles of Afro-Columbians against their social, political and economic oppression. He points out that all of us should be cognizant not only of their particular struggle, but how their struggle relates to similar battles across the African diaspora in the Americas. He notes that knowledge of said struggles empowers all of us, and gives us insight into why African religion, music and culture is more prevalent in some countries than in others. It also gives us insight into how European and African culture have merged and continue to influence each other around the globe.

What struck me about this is how timely and for me, spiritually affirming the theme of connection and interdependence is. As a man born of a Puerto Rican father and an African-American mother with Prussian, Jewish, French, Cherokee and Apache roots, I have been broadcasting this theme by posting salsa videos from Cuba, Son Fo videos from Senagal, and notes about yin and yang, etc. on social media. The point of my doing this is to broadcast to anyone who would listen that we are all inextricably connected to one another and are by definition interdependent. One of the central themes of yin and yang, a Chinese philosophical concept, is that opposites only exist in relation to each other. Is that not all of us?

I am reminded that it is our differences that cause us to rotate in the circle of yin and yang, and that we all have elements of our opposite within us. We exist only in relation to each other. Our connection is spiritual by nature, and well beyond the concepts and false walls of our limited thinking. Expand your heart, your spirit and your mind.

The struggles of Afro-Columbians to gain recognition in their society and culture is no different than the struggle of Afro-Peruvians who asked my Fulbright colleagues and I for assistance in doing the same thing in their country. They didn't just see us as black and white, they saw us as Americans, with a particular history and struggle of our own which could inform them and guide their actions today. One of my colleagues wrote an essay of his own entitled: "The Disappeared," which documented the nearly complete disappearance of Afro-Peruvians from popular culture and mainstream society. Henry Louis Gates depicts the story of African descendants throughout the Americas in the PBS documentary "Black in Latin America," which explores these themes. Tomás Fernández Robaina writes an essay about the disappearance of Afro-Columbians from their popular culture and society. This is karma.

There is no cause without effect. The fact that we are almost never conscious of the full impact of that effect doesn't bar us from the responsibility for it. You don't have to have brown skin to read the article mentioned here. You don't have to have brown skin to learn from it. *Reach out.* Know your roots. Where do you fall within the circle?

THE DANGER OF LOSING OUR CONNECTION

On February 1, 2011, I read a disturbing article in the New York Daily News about seven teenage bullies attacking a 13 year old boy in Pennsylvania. The included video brought home the sheer brutality of the attack.

See the original article here. http://www.nydailynews.com/news/national/teens-arrested-posting-youtube-video-beating-13-year-old-boy-hanging-tree-article-1.137868

As I watched the video, I couldn't help but wonder what would make kids be so cruel to one another. I mean, teasing another kid is one thing. We've all done that. But hanging another kid from a tree? And hanging him by his jacket from a fence? And dragging him through the snow, punching and kicking him along the way?

Then it struck me. That level of cruelty can only exist when we've completely forgotten our connections to one another. This happens when we don't understand that what we do has an impact not only on the person we're doing it to, but on a host of others connected by a web of relationships. Did those kids think about the impact they were having on this boy? His future interactions with others? (It's amazing, isn't it, how negative behaviors continue to manifest in future relationships. Raise your hand if you know what I'm talking about). Did they think about his mother, or the rest of his family, and how this impacts them? As a father, I can't imagine what I would have done had I seen a gang of kids doing that to one of my daughters. But I can tell you here and now that it would have gotten *ugly*. (You just don't attack a parent's children like that and expect to get away with it).

That thought brings me back to parents. What are the parents of these kids teaching them? Perhaps they're doing all they can to teach them the right things about love, honor and respect for one another. But as parents, do they not know that the lessons aren't taking hold? Or, worse yet, are they teaching them this kind of hatred?

I wrote this to remind everyone that not knowing our connections to and responsibilities for one another is inherently dangerous. It brings about our most base nature, and leads us away from the American promise of life, liberty, and the pursuit of happiness. Parents stand up!! We've got to do better than this.

CHAPTER 6

Achieving with Others (Team Building)

"Coming together is a beginning. Keeping together is progress. Working together is success." - Henry Ford

"Michael, if you can't pass, you can't play." - Coach Dean Smith to Michael Jordan in his freshman year

"A single arrow is easily broken, but not ten in a bundle." - Japanese proverb

Author's Notes:

According to Wikipedia, "team building is a philosophy of job design in which employees are viewed as members of interdependent teams instead of as individual workers…. It generally sits within the theory and practice of organizational development, but can also be applied to sports teams, school groups, and other contexts." As a former non-profit Executive Director, I've found that team building is the fulcrum upon which one moves from personal experience and knowledge to positive impact on others. One needs wisdom and knowledge to lead others, but team building relies on many subtle issues, such as one's ability to transfer knowledge in a meaningful way, and knowing the members of the team well enough to know what emotional and motivational buttons to push for each.

Using the lessons of connecting to others culturally and spiritually bodes well for anyone building a team. Without knowing who you are, without knowing specifically how you connect to others, and without knowing how to make those connections real for others through communication, team building is impossible. Many people I know don't think of it this way, but rely on their job titles as proof that they're ready to lead a group of diverse individuals to productive work. I want to note here that team building is very closely related to leadership development. I'll take this moment to remind you again that each chapter's topic is inherently related and are placed in a very specific order.

The Achieving With Others workshop is the one I have the most fun with. This is true because I literally run my participants through exercises designed to address the very subtle but real issues that impact team building, such as communication, bonding, articulating common goals, the power of experience, etc. This chapter is designed to walk you through those same themes, and exercise your mind in a way that gets you to think about your ability to move others in common directions and with common purpose.

The Blogs

I wrote "How To Make Change" as an answer to a question posed to me by someone on a social media site. The question was posed to me in such a direct manner and required such a fundamental-yet-nuanced answer that I had to take quite some time to consider it. I was surprised to note that nobody had asked me how to make change within a community before. As much as I've discussed the elements of it, I'd never considered this answer as a whole. Once I wrote the blog post, I was grateful for the question, because I saw myself grow in maturity and purpose before my own eyes. It always amazes me how much we can push each other to learn through direct, honest dialogue.

"Fire Ants Can Give A Workshop On Teamwork" was written as a response to an incredible magazine article that demonstrated not only the power of working together as a unit, but that one doesn't need a large, complicated and sophisticated brain to work well with others. Go figure! After reading the article, I thought long and hard about the issues that keep us from achieving objectives with others. I remembered walking by the water cooler and noticing how quickly the three or four colleagues gathered there fell into a hush. I remembered being the front office staff person quietly seething as "the boss" walked out early with briefcase in hand, thinking that he was heading home. What I didn't know, of course, was that he was heading to yet another meeting, with a dinner meeting scheduled after that, and that he wouldn't get home until long after I did. I also remembered with amusement that my staff would give me those same looks when I walked out the door as Executive Director.

Here we are, these complicated, intelligent, high-achieving human beings, floundering and fumbling as we try to overcome hatred and petty jealousies to work with one another. Meanwhile, the simple but unerringly focused ants lead us by example....

The Questions

I hereby challenge you to honestly think about the issues you face that hinder you from working with others as effectively as you can. Do you ever succumb to petty jealousy? Do you ever have difficulty communicating your thoughts and feelings? Do you see your "teammates" as dolts and nincompoops you'd rather be rid of? Have you ever considered that the dolt may be you? (If you've never had a "dolt" moment, please raise your hand).

This is it folks, the linchpin. This is the part where you get to start turning your inner knowledge into outward impact. Enjoy the blogs and I'll see you at the Epilogue.

100th POST

I wanted to take a moment to commemorate the 100th post of Champions' Blog.

I find that this is a moment to sit back and reflect on everything that's led to the creation and development of this vehicle by which I've shared so many personal thoughts with you.

For one thing, I want to point out that much of what's brought this about was profound pain and disappointment. That may sound strange to you at first, but my experience has been that great things often come from terrible trials. I would love to tell this heartwarming story about how I knew all along that I would write something called Champions' Blog or a book called Broadcast Your Inner Champion about self-awareness, faith, attitude & success, spiritual connection & responsibility, cultural connection, relationship building, achieving with others, leadership development, parenting and community impact. I would love to tell you that I had all this figured out and knew exactly what to say to all of you all along.

But, if I hadn't gone through anything, if I had not experienced trials and tribulations regarding each of those topics, what could I possibly say to any of you that would be informative? How could I possibly understand anyone who shared with me his/her pain, and who needed advise on how to overcome it? How could I have the insight to create The Berlack Method to personal development? I'm here, on my 100th post of Champions' Blog, to tell you that I didn't just read all this stuff in a book.

I've lived it.

And I continue to live it. How many of you would be surprised to know that, 100 posts into this, I've been thrust right back into my oldest challenge: faith vs. fear? Would you be surprised to learn that I moved forward with a plan to find work that would support me and my two daughters, only to experience the single worst relationship (with my direct supervisor, no less) on the job that I've ever experienced? Would you understand my pain if I told you that the job didn't last, and that my fear of financial ruin has run smack dab into my faith that God has both my back and The Plan? Would you understand if I told you that my faith compels me to focus on my purpose, and leave the "hows" and "whys" to Him? Would you understand my relief when I told you that once I gave my worries to Him, people near and far, people both familiar and unknown to me, stood by my side and opened opportunities that allowed me to survive my trials?

Would you understand my overwhelming emotions as I sat in church the next Sunday as my pastor gave an impassioned sermon on (of all people in the Bible...) Job? And do you understand when I tell you that I completely got the point of the sermon when my pastor highlighted that before Job could even speak to The Most High, God put him in check by asking a few questions of His own? Questions like: "Where were you when I laid the foundation of the Earth?"

Job took a big step back. And on this 100th post, so will I.

I'm taking a step back to remember that I can't achieve anything alone. First and foremost, God has seen me through every trial. I've fallen, but I've never hit the ground....

Also, I sit back to remember that for every accomplishment I've obtained, God had people surrounding me to help. Windows closed but doors were opened. People with gifts I don't possess gave them to me willingly and cheerfully. Even the website I'm typing this blog on was provided by someone who answered when He told her: "build this for him." (Thank you again Dr. Diva Verdun for listening)! I can't make this stuff up....

That brings me to the point of this post.

With all the trials I've gone through, and with all the trials I continue to endure, I must say thank you. Thank you God for always cupping me in Your loving hands. Thank you to all who have helped me on this journey. The list of people I have to thank really is too long to place here. (Don't worry, you'll be in the book)! But you already know who you are.

I say thank you because I never achieve alone. I have God, and although they may look like ordinary people to you, I have His angels. May this post inspire someone going through a great trial today. And may s/he pass his/her gifts and blessings to others, so that they may broadcast their inner champions.

Amen.

IT'S LINSANE! TEAMWORK TRUMPS TALENT

I have to start this post by admitting: I'm a die-hard Knicks fan. To say that I am, like my fellow fanatics, long-suffering, would be stating the obvious. My beloved team last won a world championship 40 years ago. I've never actually witnessed them winning it all. Being a Giants and Yankees fan as well, this has been hard for me to take. So why still be a Knicks fan? Well, if you're a fan, then you're a fan. Thick or thin. Win or lose. What can I tell you?

What I can do is tell you how excited I've been over the last two years as the Knicks have finally made personnel moves that, in theory, should have the Knicks in title contention. We first brought in league star Amar'e Stoudemire, who, along with a cast of relative unknowns gave us a glimpse of competitive basketball for the first time in almost a decade. Then, following conventional wisdom, the Knicks did everything they could to get a second star player in Carmelo Anthony.

The problem? The Knicks, in my humble opinion, gave up too many of their lesser-known, team-first players. With a tremendous amount of talent, and little depth, the Knicks did something surprising: they struggled. In fact, after the Knicks acquired Carmelo, they finished the year 14-14. They were then swept in the playoffs - four straight losses and out. The next year, after getting another star player in Tyson Chandler, the Knicks ignited their fan base again. We were all *finally* not only excited, but expectant of watching a legitimate title contender. This was it! We finally had the star power we needed to win! Fans were high-fiving each other and dreaming of a championship before the first jump ball was tossed. So what happened?

We start the year 9-15. Losers. Again. For all of our talent, it turned out that our stars did not mesh well together. For one, our biggest star, Carmelo Anthony, holds the ball for long periods while the rest of his teammates stand around waiting for magic to happen. And it doesn't. At least not consistently. Knick fans began yelling for the coach to be fired. We were booing our team during games, and we were absolutely frustrated by this tease of talent. So what happens?

For various extremely unfortunate reasons, our two biggest stars miss a week of action. And then it hit. Linsanity. An undrafted, unheralded player named Jeremy Lin, who spent the first part of the year at the end of the Knick bench, via Harvard University, no less...finally got his chance to play with our roster depleted. And wouldn't you know it? He leads the Knicks to five straight wins. Not only does he light the scoreboard up in creative ways we never knew he had in him, he makes his *teammates* better by passing the ball to them so that *they* score. Bench players who were afterthoughts are now filling the basket with ease. The energy in Madison Square Garden is electric again as players are now diving on the floor for loose balls, hounding their opponents on defense, and running to the basket *knowing* that Lin will get them the ball. If a Knick gets knocked to the floor, all of his teammates run to help him up.

And the entire sports nation caught Linsanity. How can you not root for a guy who comes out of Harvard with an economics degree? How can you not root for a guy who'd been cut by two different teams in the previous year, and who was about to be cut from the Knicks before he exploded onto the scene? How can you not root for a guy who, with his picture now on every newspaper back page across the country, and who's given America a new word for its lexicon, answers reporters' questions about how he did it by stating that this is not about him. He goes on to say that his teammates aren't getting the credit they deserve. And that we should all see the hard work and sacrifice his fellow former no-names put in night after night. And for a guy who has been given credit for energizing a team and an entire city, all he does is smile and say it's his teammates that energize him.

And there it is.

So here's a small bit of advice to our stars. From a long-suffering fan who's seen talent come and go: when you step on the court, leave your ego in the locker room and get with the Linsanity. If you want to win a championship, score when you can as is your talent, but give up the ball and your energy to your teammates when you can't. Be selfless, and make sure your teammates get the credit they deserve, even if you are the star.

No, you may not get the spotlight. But you just might get that ring, and add to the Linsane idea that teamwork trumps talent.

HOW TO MAKE CHANGE

On one of my social network pages, a friend asked me how to effectively institute change as an individual or as part of organizations. My first thought? "What a complicated question!" Many ideas raced through my mind, and I quickly realized that I would need a moment to organize them all. I stepped away from the computer and engaged in another activity so that I could allow my thoughts to marinate and I could thoroughly absorb the question and appreciate all of its nuances. (I do this often when I want to think. It's amazing how clear your mind can become while walking the dog, listening to music or cleaning the house).

Here was my response:

1) I think we have to start with the ideas that <name> and <name> have already posited. We each need to get rid of the ego, pompousness, jealousy, etc. and really want ALL to shine.
2) ALL who are willing to work to help the community are qualified. If I'm looking for a brain surgeon to operate on me, then I want to see degrees, experience, etc. The community is different. To wit: I'm a Fulbright Scholar with a Master's Degree, but all the people in the community I've serviced care about is that I'm also born and raised in the South Bronx to a single parent, and I know what it's like to go to bed hungry. I can understand what they're going through. YOU CAN'T FAKE THE FUNK!
3) We need to all do our research and become AWARE of each other as organizations.
4) NETWORK, NETWORK, NETWORK. By the way, refer back to number 2 on this one.
5) We must all be of the same mind that MUCH of our work is connecting our clients/participants to their past. We spend a lot of time spinning our wheels when we don't get our clients to see WHO THEY ARE, and WHY they're not only significant in this world, but CRUCIAL.
6) NETWORK, NETWORK, NETWORK. I don't have to go back to number 2, do I?
7) Our networking must include ALL aspects of life and career. We have to connect organizations to funding to politics to policy. Which brings me to the last point....
8) Poor communities must take ownership of their own issues and be willing to SELF-CORRECT! No-one can lead them to the promised land. Waiting for people in power (read that how you will) to change policy so that they lose power and give it to those that don't already have it is naive at best. That brings us back to number 5.

To that end, The Berlack Method, LLC stands willing and able to network/connect with each of you here to bring positive change to our families, our communities, our nation and our world. To find out more, visit: www.steveberlack.org. I especially encourage you to check out: TBM's description, Champions' Blog, and the video library under the "Events" tab.

Peace and Blessings,

- Steve

That's my take on making positive and effective change. What's yours?

IT'S SPELLED T.E.A.M.

One of the great things about the NBA is that fanatics, casual fans and non-fans alike tune in to the drama and excitement that is the Finals. This particular Finals was intriguing because the two teams involved (The Dallas Mavericks and The Miami Heat) were diametrically opposed in terms of makeup and style of play. Even more compelling was the fact that many fans were not just rooting for their teams, but were rooting against the Heat. Why? Because of fan hatred that was self-inflicted. The center of the firestorm against the Heat was squarely focused on LeBron James, and, in my humble opinion, for good reason.

To say that LeBron James is an exceptionally talented basketball player is an understatement in the extreme. He is arguably one of the best, particularly at this stage of his career. So when LeBron became a free agent, fans around the country had renewed hope for their franchises, and lit up social media outlets pleading for him to sign with their teams. LeBron, being a young man, took this so much to heart that he mistakenly thought that all the hoopla was about him. *It wasn't.* This is a common mistake among the young.

From every interview I've seen with LeBron, he couldn't understand why fans were so upset with him about his reality t.v.-styled one hour special he called "The Decision." That is because he never understood that by producing a one-hour special just so we could all learn who he would sign with, by making everyone wait for the prime-time "Decision," by holding teams hostage to his whim, and by holding court in his hometown hotel room as various teams traveled across the country for the privilege of grovelling at his feet, he made the entire process about *him*. This meant that he never understood why fans were excited about his free agency in the first place. They were excited for their *teams*, for the possibility of signing one of the NBA's greats so that he could wear *their* uniform. Period.

There was another glaring instance of LeBron not getting the concept of "team". When he, Dwayne Wade and Chris Bosh appeared on stage in Miami with their uniforms on, dancing to music and smoke machines like they were in a scene from a bad, B-rated sports movie, it apparently never occurred to them that they should include the rest of the *team* in the news conference. What, aren't the rest of the Heat important, too? By having the three of them showboating on stage and mindlessly claiming seven or more championships, what message was Heat management sending to the rest of the Heat? Would *you* want to be a member of that team and be completely ignored in this way?

At the end of the day, (for this particular season at least), a Dallas Maverick team with one superstar and a bunch of important and relied-upon role players won the championship over three superstars and a bunch of ignored "teammates." The Mavericks became champions because a bunch of their players whose talent levels don't compare to LeBron's figured out how to step in to the game and step up at critical moments. They passed the ball, literally and figuratively, to each other at just the right times. Apparently, talent isn't everything. As Rick Carlisle, the Mavericks coach stated after being awarded the championship trophy:

"We don't jump high, and we don't run fast, but we play well together."

What a concept. The old mantra bears repeating here, because it is so tried and true:

There is no 'I' in TEAM.

Corny? Maybe. Old-fashioned? Most definitely. But "team" is a concept even a megastar like LeBron can't conquer.

TEAMWORK MAKES THE NIGHTMARE END

I've heard many people use the catchphrase "teamwork makes the dream work" to capture the power and effectiveness of unified effort. My workshops on the subject speak to this. I often find that the staff members who benefit most from this particular workshop are those who explore and examine who they are first as individuals (and the issues that accompany them) before they explore how they can become working members of effective teams. Often, that self-examination is a painful but necessary step to the subjugation of one's individual personality for the benefit of the unit.

That brings me to an issue I seem to be hitting lately while interacting with different people, and to a rather disturbing article I read early this morning....

Politics is always a tricky issue to debate. Like sex and religion, politics engenders fervent beliefs and opinions. Because of this, it is often difficult to engage in discourse with someone of an opposite opinion without the conversation degrading into shouting matches and name-calling. However, who reading this can think of a team s/he has been on that didn't have members of varying opinions? (And I mean any team: family, close friends, athletic teams, co-workers, church members, etc.). Considering that it seems to be my season of debating politics lately, I will throw this out for consideration: as Americans, if we are not all a part of a huge team, then what are we?

As I can recall Richard Pryor saying in his standup: "This is *America*, Jack!" Though we may not be a true melting pot, we are certainly a tossed salad. We have different languages, world views, communities, family structures, livelihoods, and the list goes on and on. To say that Americans differ on issues such as limits and roles of government, national healthcare, how to fix public education, the Middle East wars and the like would be such an understatement as to almost miss the point. As part of the American team it's our *job* to differ from one another, debate the issues at hand, *listen* to one another, and...with some grace and a little thing called *respect*...we can learn from one another and make decisions about policy that strengthens America as a whole.

As Americans, what side of the aisle one leans towards is inconsequential, as long as what I've stated above holds true. Which brings me to the article I read this morning. Mark Williams, Chairman and Founder of The Tea Party Express wrote an article called "Tea Party Must Take Over GOP" that was…well…disturbing. I have no doubt that Mr. Williams loves America and wishes nothing but the best for our country. As I've written earlier, whether or not I agree with his politics is inconsequential. His political views make sense to me given his perspective and what I know of him. What was disturbing was his flagrant disregard for the rule of respect and open communication.

In the article, Williams calls out Independent voters as "cowards" who, by their inability to pick a side, are *the* problem with America. This is not exactly a shining example of winning new friends and influencing people. As if that weren't enough, he paints the "evil" media, Democrats and the like thus:

"Duplicitous collaborators with evil in the media, vapid talking heads, along with a collection of office holding hypocrites and on line reprobates have all descended on our way of life like a starving pack of hyenas on a fallen zebra. They smell Lady Liberty's blood and have pounced in an effort to finish us off, to extinguish free thought, speech and the lights of the Shining City on the Hill to install in their place the false god of Statism in all of its hideous forms."

Huh? Whose way of life is he talking about? And did he really call fellow Americans hyenas? What kind of debate tactic is that? And scarier still, who's *listening* to this diatribe? Oh…he didn't end there:

"Each of us must vow to recognize that the letter "D" after a politician's name is a metaphorical Mark of the Beast, inasmuch as that party is now a wholly owned subsidiary of the domestic enemy, and that to repair and make again effective the Republican Party we must each do our part to take control of that party, not step away from it."

Help me out here, people. Seriously? Democrats carry the mark of the beast? It is exactly this kind of rhetoric that is dangerous and drags the American dream kicking and screaming towards the American Nightmare.

As a child of God I stand fast in my commitment to spreading the message that we are all connected and responsible for one another. As a human being, I recognize and respect the right that all of us have to differ in opinion. As an American and veteran of the U.S. Army, I salute the same flag we all do. As an entrepreneur, I do not allow politics to interfere with our common pursuit of life, liberty and happiness.

As a teammate, I say to those who can't get their mind wrapped around a President of the U.S. who looks different than they do:

Get. Over. It.

Stay on the team, people. And pull that nightmare back to the Dream....

GUEST ON THE PHILIPPE MATTHEWS SHOW

I had the honor of being interviewed on The Philippe Matthews Show, which aired on June 1, 2011, on Blog Talk Radio. The interview was ostensibly a review of how I started The Berlack Method, LLC, its focus and structure as a personal development workshop series. However, it ultimately became a testimony of my spiritual journey. I spoke about how I came to recognize my God-given talent for public speaking, the different events that led to my founding TBM, and the many people who have blessed me to continue on my journey towards blessing others.

You can listen to the full interview by clicking here. http://ht.ly/57n7T

I say I was honored because of the tremendous gifts and life work of Philippe Matthews himself. His bio follows:

*Heralded as the "Oprah of Internet," by Co-Author of Chicken Soup for the Soul (http://bit.ly/cD6ln9), Mark Victor Hansen; Philippe Matthews is a world expert on creating, producing, and marketing Internet television shows.

In response to being called the Oprah of Internet he says, "O always comes before P! Oprah is truly my role model and media matriarch."

The Philippe Matthews Show is a trilogy internet marketing production; allowing his audience to listen to it exclusively on BlogTalk Radio, watch it exclusively on YouTube or read it on his interactive Blog.

The Philippe Matthews Show has featured such notable guests as Robert T. Kiyosaki, Dr. John F. Demartini, Russell Simmons, Marianne Williamson, Stedman Graham, Mark Victor Hansen, Robert G. Allen, Zig Ziglar and countless more.

You can watch The Philippe Matthews show here http://thepmshow.tv/

or

You can visit his YouTube Channel here. https://www.youtube.com/user/philippematthews

Thank you Philippe for a job well done and I look forward to seeing how our gifts combine to bless others.

FIRE ANTS CAN GIVE A WORKSHOP ON TEAMWORK

I often remark to my workshop participants how amazing it is where we can find life lessons, and who we can learn them from. Not only can we learn from doctoral-level educators at Ivy League schools, we can learn from people in any walk of life and with little to no formal education. An article in the May 13, 2011 issue of *The Week* magazine, "Fire Ants' Cohesive Genius," demonstrates that even animals, including insects with infinitesimally small brains, can provide us with serious life lessons.

Researchers from the Georgia Institute of Technology have discovered that fire ants are teamwork gurus that we should all learn from.

To wit:

"When a colony is washed out by flood, thousands of the insects quickly assemble into a tightly woven pancake-shaped raft that can float for months without a single ant drowning. 'Together they form this really complex material' that water can't get through, lead researcher Nathan Mlot tells **Nature.com***. You could even mold the ant cluster 'into a ball and toss it up in the air, and all the ants would stay together.'"*

Now, can someone explain to me why *homo sapiens* don't do that? Not only does the ants' phenomenal feat of teamwork help each individual survive, it helps the colony survive harsh environments that would tear us poor humans asunder. Isn't survival the ultimate goal of teamwork? And is that not the very reason why Fortune 500 companies spend significant percentages of their budgets to train their staff on topics as fundamental as teamwork? Do they not spend their money so that the companies themselves can survive in tough times? And with all that money spent, how do we respond when our society (or our companies) are proverbially tossed into the air?

Think about it. How did we as a nation respond to Hurricane Katrina? Did we hold tightly together and fall as a unit? Or did we, as a whole... fall apart and fall as individuals, weakened by our disassociation with one another? How did we respond to the earthquake in Haiti? How did we respond to 9/11?

The short answer: we responded much like ants would - we stuck together. All of a sudden, political, cultural and racial barriers failed to keep us from seeing each other as part of one human race, and there was story after story of individuals and groups stepping above and beyond to assist any and all in need. TEAMWORK.

The long answer: as time wore on, and the novelty of the catastrophe (our being tossed in the air) wore off, we forgot the sublime lessons of connection and oneness. We fell back into the traps of politics, greed and disassociation: blaming one another for how/when we responded (or if we responded at all). Money destined for those most in need disappeared into the pockets of...? And as the memories (and emotions) of the catastrophes faded, we moved on to the next one....

So I invite you: reinvigorate your commitment to all around you. Realize (if even for the first time) - that a baby born in Sri Lanka this morning is part of our "pancake network," and helps us grow stronger and survive as a unit as s/he latches on and contributes his/her strength and talents.

And remember, when we get tossed into the air again (and we will) - we all land safely if we just *hang on* to one another....

HUMILITY BEFORE TEAMWORK BEFORE LEADERSHIP

It will be 25 years this October that I first came brim-to-brim with Drill Sergeant Herndon of South Carolina. The fact that after all these years I still remember his name and where he's from says a lot about the man. He was about 5'10" tall and just about as wide...all muscle.

I didn't know he existed when I boarded the bus from Ft. Hamilton in Brooklyn, New York, on my way to basic training in Ft. Dix, New Jersey. I still remember the nervous laughter we shared as we rode towards what surely would be tough training. We cracked jokes, we smiled and laughed, and even the driver chimed in, as happy as a lark.

That changed when we saw the highway sign that read: "Ft. Dix - 2 miles." After the smokers on the bus partook of several cigarettes and the bus partook of silence, we pulled up to the staging area. Our once happy and conciliatory driver shape-shifted into an ornery, gravel-voiced ogre, barking at us to "get the hell off my bus! MOVE!!!" That was nothing. As we all hauled it off the bus, we lined up as per instructions, and as fate would have it, I was lined up right in front Drill Sgt. Herndon. So guess what he did?

Without missing a beat, he did what Americans hate profoundly: he completely invaded my personal space. He placed the brim of his "brown round" right against my soon to be immaculately coiffed head, and spewed something about me being the sorriest example of human existence he'd ever seen. (I'm giving you the PG-rated version. You can guess the rest of what he said). He then did something hilarious. He called me "Willie." He never bothered to ask my name, but from then on I was "Willie." Period.

For some reason I thought this was the funniest thing I'd ever heard at the time, but I knew better than to laugh. Mamma didn't raise no fool. Thus began my first lesson: learn when to shut the (add expletive here, if you'd like) up, and quickly assess who is the lion and who is the antelope in any given situation.

Through the years, as I made my way upward through both the non-profit and public school system ladder, I thought about that moment often. I always wondered why some of my colleagues struggled so much with being part of a team. I wondered why the organization would suffer in productivity because of a simple lack of communication, or a small missed detail. And I realized, after years of experience, that there are people out there who lack the fundamental skill taught so well by Drill Sergeant Herndon: humility.

I eventually came to the simple but life-altering conclusion that before one can be effective as a member of a team, s/he has to first be clear that it's okay to realize that sometimes you just ain't all that. That in turn allows one to place the needs of others ahead of one's own goals. Which in turn allows one to understand that being responsible for the success of the team is at least as important as being responsible for oneself, if not more. And that in turn leads one to see that before one can ever hope to effectively lead others, s/he must have mastered the concept of team. Too many of us never get that lesson, or place the elements of this equation in the wrong order.

I don't know if we all need to meet a Drill Sergeant Herndon, but we all need to learn this lesson if we're to become successful: as individuals, as a community, as a nation, and as a people.

What is *your* humility meter reading these days?

CHAPTER 7

Relationship Building (Personal)

"Man may have discovered fire, but women discovered how to play with it." — Candace Bushnell, *Sex and the City*

"The meeting of two personalities is like the contact of two chemical substances: if there is any reaction, both are transformed." — C.G. Jung

"When you stop expecting people to be perfect, you can like them for who they are." — Donald Miller

Author's Notes:

According to the Merriam-Webster dictionary online, a relationship is: 1) the way in which two or more people, groups, countries, etc., talk to, behave toward, and deal with each other 2) a romantic or sexual friendship between two people 3) the way in which two or more people or things are connected. When I read this definition I was reminded of why I like to start each of my workshops (and the chapters of this book) by defining the themes discussed. It is specifically because of the fundamental nature of these themes that we often overlook key concepts. Because we each miss different elements of the definition, we often argue over something as theoretically simple as what we should do or how we should behave within our relationships. Some of the biggest arguments I've seen occurred because "he should know this" or because "she just doesn't get me."

When I think of my relationships - platonic, romantic and familial, I get flashes of memories and emotions tied to my dealings with people around me. I remember feelings of complete peace interspersed with terse arguments and frustration. I remember moments of awe as I've said "yeah, me too!" and moments of awe (is that the word I'm looking for?) as I've said "oh, I'd *never* do that!" But reading this particular definition reminds me that at the heart of any relationship is the *connection* that relationship represents. I've been reminded that relationships are the manifestations of our move from focus on self to impact on others. And that's what this book is all about.

Relationship building is intimately tied to team building and achieving with others. In order to properly build a team, be it comprised of co-workers or family members, one must spend a lot of time and effort getting to know what makes those nearby "tick." As social creatures, it is imperative that we understand that our individual happiness and success is tied directly to the happiness and success of others. Having a strong sense of self mentally, emotionally, and spiritually makes it much easier to make connections to others and nurture the relationships that grow from them. Being at peace with oneself through self-awareness (being able to fully answer "who am I?" and "to whom do I belong?") allows one to put aside ego when considering the needs of others, and makes establishing and maintaining relationships not only easier, but makes them more satisfying.

I submit to you that holding on to ego and focusing on oneself makes the core elements of relationship building – communication, active listening, transparency of intentions, respect, etc. almost impossible. It is therefore by building relationships that we receive our greatest chance to "broadcast our inner champions." By shining the light of our self-awareness, connecting to others through focus on similarities, and building relationships with those around us, we begin the process of moving from inward self to outward impact. This is, indeed, a process, and, like any process, it can be mastered.

THE BLOGS

This chapter took the biggest toll on me to write. In order to write it, I had to experience tremendous pain in my personal relationships. People close to me betrayed me. Those who loved me turned on me. Those who held my heart in their hands squashed it. And, most painful of all, I let myself down with my own mistakes and horrible actions. Yet, I've found that this pain has also led to tremendous victories. Hard lessons learned by me became the focus of my workshops, and thereby helped others. The pain I've experienced also helped me to fully appreciate the many wonderful pleasant and peaceful moments that my relationships have brought. And I've learned three overarching lessons: 1) my greatest relationships are those that have endured many obstacles over the years and have remained strong. 2) our past relationships serve to inform us how to build our future ones 3) We all share the pain and pleasure of connection, and ultimately, it is our awareness of this that allows our connections to deepen.

The blog that captures my lessons learned more than any other is "Look-A-Likes." More synopsis than a reflection on any individual, it was written after I spent a day just thinking about the many crazy and wonderful romantic relationships I've experienced. I spent a lot of time considering how naïve I've been in my life, and how my initial lack of awareness about my "non-negotiables" doomed many of them before they began. My mind is way to diffuse to hold detailed lists, but as the day went on I began to realize how much I'd grown through each relationship, and that I maintained a much sharper picture of "her" and what she looks like as I got older. I also realized that the sharper my image of "her" became, the more I began to run into women who "looked" like her. When I grow up, I'll let you know the degree to which "she" ticked off on my list.

"Tissues From The Sky" is my ode to Grandpa. He was my hero and my role model. Born in 1914, he still wore a suit and tie with matching fedora wherever he went by the time I came along. He never said anything about it, but he showed me how a man should represent himself and his family in the street.

Even as I type this, one of my earliest memories of him is flashing before me. I was about 4 years old, and Grandpa and I were walking down the street near our apartment on a hot, sunny afternoon. As always, Grandpa held my hand and walked just fast enough to challenge me to keep up. We were passing a group of older kids that were part of a local gang. They wore denim jackets with the sleeves cut off, and on the back of each was a picture of a skull and crossbones, with the words "Savage Skulls" emblazoned on banners above and below. One of them said "Hey Mr. Berlack." Grandpa looked over, smiled, and said "Hey boys. This is my grandson, Steven. You make sure nobody bothers him." "Okay, Mr. Berlack, we got him." I asked him who they were. Grandpa told me that two of them had jumped him some time before. He not only beat them both, but put them in the hospital. He visited them, and instead of pressing charges, he decided to help the boys by assisting them with finding jobs and connecting them with friends to help them with other family issues, etc. He said that ever since then, he and the gang had an "understanding." He said that if I ever came across others who were struggling, I should never look down on them, but should help them and care for them. That was Grandpa.

I can still smell the cherry tobacco from the pipe he smoked all the time. To this day, if I wear a suit and tie, there's a good chance I'll top it off with a matching fedora. "Tissues From The Sky" got its name because as serious as Grandpa could be about representing the family and social issues, he was a big kid at heart who used to play with my cousin Sharon and I daily. I play with my girls the same way.

As for relationships, I still maintain that Grandma and Grandpa were the funniest couple I ever met. They fussed and loved their way through decades together. When I talk about building relationships, I always think of them.

QUESTIONS FOR YOU

As you read this chapter, consider:

1) How many relationships have you had in your life (platonic, romantic and familial)?
2) What role do you play in the building of your relationships?
3) What's been the greatest challenge for you in building relationships?
    a. If there are similar challenges throughout, what's the common denominator?
4) What have you learned from your prior relationships, and how does that help you in your current ones?
5) What's negotiable for you in relationships, and what's not?
6) What are you teaching others about what you've learned?

I pray you enjoy the blogs, and have not gone through as much pain in your relationships as I have. If you have, then I pray that you've learned as much as I have or more. At the end of the day, maintaining a positive attitude (remember that chapter?) about what you've experienced will allow for richer, fuller relationships in the future.

See you at the Epilogue.

WHAT MEN WANT

As President of The Berlack Method, I've participated as either a facilitator or panelist for many forums and community events on relationships. Some of the most memorable ones occurred with all-female audiences and all-male panelists. No matter what questions were asked, invariably, the one ladies wanted answered most of all was: "What do men want?"

Now, no man in his right mind would ever say he represents all men and can tell ladies what men want. We can only give our perspectives based on our individual desires, experiences, etc. Even though we male panelists were smart enough and experienced enough to solve the issue and proclaim *the answer* to all ladies (sarcasm inserted), the issue keeps coming up for me in my discussions with women.

So I thought about it. And I remembered that years ago, I wrote exactly what I wanted in an online dating profile. (Yes, I went there...WHAT)?!? I was able to dig it up, and here's what I wrote:

I'm looking for a woman who can flow with me in any situation. She has no problem with going to the theater to catch a play with me on Thursday, checking out the new jazz lounge on Friday, then settling down on the couch with me on Sunday for some football. She's a nurturer by nature, and sees cooking as her way of expressing her love. She can't go a day without laughing, and can joke with me about Austin Powers right after discussing the war in Iraq. She can stand up for herself with anyone, but does NOT sweat the small stuff. She is keenly aware of (and comfortable with) her femininity and sexuality, but her wit is her weapon of choice. She's the type of woman who speaks pleasantly to the cleaning lady at the hotel, all the while giving me that side glance that says: "Wait 'til we get alone in that room!"

I look back at that description years later and think, "yeah, that's still it." So there's a few things I'd like to point out to the ladies:

First, notice that there's nothing said about financial status. I've heard a lot of women say that they come across men who are intimidated by their success. My retort: those are males you're meeting, not men. There's a difference. 21st Century men have evolved enough to understand that our economy generally demands two incomes in the household, and whoever makes the most is just detail.

Second, the woman described above is one who can wear many hats and go seamlessly from one situation to another with her man. In my opinion, most women do this naturally. It just seems to be their nature. Of course, I'm speaking anecdotally, but women I know are masters at bringing home the bacon *and* frying it up in the pan. Believe it or not, most men really appreciate that in their women. (See note above about males vs. men).

Third, the most important word in my description above is…wait for it… nurturing. I don't care what anyone tells you, I can say unequivocally that every man I've ever met (including me) wants to be nurtured! I describe what I mean by mentioning how she sees cooking. It's not a chore to endure. It's not something to delegate (although men of the house today must know how to cook as well). What's most important is how she *feels* about cooking. It represents opportunity. And love. If their women are tearing it up in the kitchen, men will tell their boys in the middle of happy hour with dancing girls all around: "Uh, dude, I gotta get home. Baby's cooking my favorite tonight!"

Obviously, this is just my take, and this is a rather simplified answer. However, there are some challenges that I think women should be mindful of.

Challenge #1: gender roles. My description above doesn't account for this issue, but I have written about how changing gender roles have impacted our relationships. To wit:

Men are tired of opening doors for one lady and receiving thanks and smiles in return, then opening doors for another lady and getting cussed out because "I don't need no man to open doors for me."

That is NOT some story or anecdote to be debated, that is REAL, with REAL men telling it!

The issue is that men and women aren't "seeing" each other because we've gotten gender roles TWISTED. In Grandpa's day, the good news was that there was NO debate about roles - the men brought home the bacon and protected and secured their families. The bad news was that that meant that the women STAYED HOME and took care of nurturing the family and keeping the home together.

Now ladies, since you've ventured out into what used to be commonly accepted as the man's world, which you have EVERY RIGHT to do, then you must understand that the challenge is to do so while still honoring your man and his position as the leader of the family. And frankly, there are women out there who aren't good at that at all. And men, to help the ladies out, we must step our game up!

Honestly, both men and women have a lot of work to do. But this is about what men want, so I'll address the ladies: bringing home the bacon and frying it up is all good, but you still must know that what makes men tick has never changed. If you don't treat your man like a *man*, then you'll always wind up with something less. While you marinate on that, let me bring up the next challenge, which is related:

Challenge #2 (ladies): your tongue. Every woman I've spoken to about this acknowledged that intuitively they knew that their tongues were their greatest weapons against men. I know women who are tenth-degree Black Belts in "tongue lashing." They can cut a man (or woman) down to size just by unleashing that devilish organ. And they often do so, unfortunately, without thinking about it. Ladies, if you want to know what men feel about your use of the tongue as a weapon, check out this Proverb:

"It's better to live alone in the corner of an attic than with a quarrelsome wife in a lovely home." - Proverbs 25:24

I just can't put it any better than that.

So to summarize, men in general want different things depending on their individual tastes. But we *all* want to be nurtured to some degree and we all want you to remember that we're still the hunters and village leaders our club-bearing forefathers were. As a last piece of advice:

Men: *man up!!* Women: *lady down*: there are leaders coming through. And if that statement hurt a little bit inside, then maybe you have some self-examination to do.

Ladies? Gentlemen? Your thoughts?

LOOK-A-LIKES

When we are young ("and dumb," as my Drill Sergeant used to say), the biggest obstacle to our finding love is ourselves. We fly recklessly from one encounter and conquest to another. At best, we have fun and explore; at worst we hurt each other irreparably as we tear through each other's hearts.

But tear through we must. Being young, we often find, rightfully so, that we're not ready for long-term commitments. We engage in the battle of establishing ourselves in the world, searching for the "truth" of self-discovery. We travel the four corners of our individual worlds, learning and growing the whole time. And time is the rub. We have none for committing the energy needed to build lasting romantic relationships with others.

As we get older, however, and if we're smart, we use our experiences to paint the picture of who we're looking for. More often than not, we know who we want in the future by who didn't work for us in the past. We learn to read the signs. We discover that someone who says X today means that Y will happen tomorrow. Or next month. Or next year. We find out that a potential mate who disrespects the waiter at our favorite restaurant has issues that will soon spill onto us. A slapped face today almost always means a broken rib tomorrow, no matter how many times we hear "I'm sorry" and "I'll never do it again." A mate who cusses us behind closed doors soon cusses us in front of family and friends.

And so we continue to hone the list. S/he must look like "this." S/he must have a job. S/he must have a good relationship with the family. Etc., etc. Some of us wind up with quite the extensive list. And some of us get so good at knowing the list that we can spout it off without hesitation and at a moment's notice.

And, finally, older and more mature, with established list in hand, we're finally ready to look for Mr./Ms. Right. And that's when we discover the next great challenge.

The Look-A-Likes.

As we've matured, so have they. As life piles dirt on our diamonds, it has done so with theirs as well. We have issues, and so do they. And as we continue to meet Mr./Ms. Potential, we engage in long-term, emotional relationships. At best, we learn and grow together, but at worst, the garbage bags we haul around with us from our previous experiences smash the mirror of our relationships. We find that Mr./Ms. Potential looks exactly like Mr./Ms. Right. We are exulted because we finally found it! Love! The One! S/he has (almost) everything ticked off on our list! This is it!

And then it happens....

An old wound you've overlooked and that you've had no part in inflicting explodes all over you. Mr./Ms. Potential moves gracefully to Mr./Ms. Right before crashing and burning before your very eyes into the valley of Mr./Ms. Ex. Sometimes, the signs come so early you don't even get to engage at all. Mr./Ms. Look-A-Like blows your list away, until s/he speaks. And you sit there with that flabbergasted look on your face. (Raise your hand if you know what I'm talking about). Or, your heart skips a beat as Look-A-Like walks by, then does that one *nasty* habit you just can't stand. You sit there, thinking: "Okay, that really might be just a small thing. Maybe I can get over that." Then Look-A-Like speaks. (See above).

And so, you keep searching, list and pen in hand, ready to start ticking off at the sight of the next Look-A-Like.

The moral of the story?

Our lists are like plans. And plans are just guides. If you've lived long enough, you already know that your plans are just a way to make God laugh. So go ahead, have your list. At best it will guide you through your Look-A-Likes. And you can't even have a Look-A-Like if you don't know who you're looking for in the first place. Just know that Mr./Ms. Right will never be The Perfect One. In the end, The One for you might be all over your list, or may not be on it at all. But if you're blessed, s/he'll tick off perfectly on His.

THE LOVE-PAIN

Our emanating lines, born from the very essence of our minds, our hearts, our souls; lied apart.

And there was pain. For it is the very nature of our lines to link.

Our lines linked for reasons we think we understand. (But of course we don't). Yet because you are you, and I am I, our essence intertwined.

And there was pain. For at the time, *we* did not know who *us* would be, and our confusion was the barrier that prevented the utter miracle of two separate entities becoming a true one.

Now, though we have criss-crossed in so many ways and at so many different times, other forces will pry my mind, my heart and my soul away from yours. The seal of time is broken, and we face…

Pain. For although hindsight is twenty-twenty, foresight is totally blind.

Now, our lines lie apart again, with history the only hint of our possible future happiness. But there are many dangers. There are sharp and grinding forces that rip to shreds the essence of our souls. And there are other lines, which, due to their very nature, might intertwine with ours and cause *us* to fall short. The thought of this possibility brings even more…

Pain. But it is this very pain, this love-pain, that gives me the desire to see the day when our emanating lines, the essence of our souls, not only intertwine, but truly become...

ONE.

TISSUES FROM THE SKY

Weston Benjamin Berlack 1914-1997

I was ten years old. Laying on my stomach. My chin resting on my hands. On a soft, comfortable bed. A bed so large I could swim from one side to the other. There was an old, familiar scent in my nose. Something like apple pie and old wood furniture. Familiar knick-knacks surrounded me; old pewter figurines and a worn, red pin-cushion on the burnished bureau. My mind was blessed with ease. I was home.

I was watching an old t.v. show. A comedy. I was lost in that daze that kids fall into when watching a show they liked. Between states, hearing and not hearing, seeing and not seeing, lazily and happily passing the day.

Then my bliss was shattered by the force of something hitting my head. <<THWAP!>> Out of my peripheral vision, I see a small yellow ball bounce off my head and careen towards the wall, its flight halted with a loud, wet-sucking thud. And it sticks. I look to the wall, and see five more yellow balls, in various stages of drying, testaments to the persistence of my tormentor. Peals of laughter spring forth behind me, and running footsteps pound the floor. I smile as I hear both fade into the background.

"Grandma!" I yell. And she's off in a flash, taking off from the kitchen, broom in hand, protecting her baby. Each sweep of the broom is embellished with a syllable from her mouth: "DID-N'T-I-TELL-YOU-TO-LEAVE-THAT-BOY-A-LONE?" Funny thing: the angrier she got, ("Lord, he's worse than the baby!"), the louder he would laugh. A howling, infectious laugh that would stay with me forever.

Now that he's gone, I realize how much I miss those tissues bouncing off my head. I realize that he threw those little yellow balls to tell me how much he enjoyed my company, how happy he was to have me there, to know me, to love me, to share laughter with me.

And now, no matter where I go, no matter what I do, I know you're with me Grandpa, 'cause I feel tissues from the sky, bouncing off my head. I live my life with laughter fading into the background.

WE CAN ALL LEARN FROM BABY

Over the last couple of days, there has been a great debate raging in The Berlack Method Group on Facebook. The topic that has everyone in a tizzy is interracial dating. As of this writing, there have been over two hundred posts to the thread. Because of the nature of this particular group, the debate has been respectful. However, the opinions have ranged all over the map.

As one might imagine, the group members have been passionate and emphatic about articulating their perspectives. Some believe that there is no reason to ever date outside one's race, some have articulated that Black men, in particular, who date outside their race do so specifically to run away from their culture, while others have stated simply that love is love, and who are we to deny a member of the human race the opportunity to find and express his/her love for someone?

I read the thread with great interest. I made a point of biding my time so as not to influence the discussion. After a significant amount of posts had been made, I jumped in and gave, in general, this perspective: we've forgotten to place God in the equation. We're so busy arguing earthly and historical points, that we're forgetting that we're all made in God's image, and we are all his children. If He loves us, who are we to deny love to anyone, irrespective of our different races, ethnicities and cultures.

I thought I was quite smart in my points, thank you very much. However, someone posted something that caused me to pause and consider his point. It was a stretch for me to assume that all involved in the thread were Christians. I thought that was an honest and eye-opening retort. So I stopped and thought about that for a while, turning the idea over in my mind. After some time, my response was to reiterate a quote which for me sums up the tagline: broadcast your inner champion. I typed: I cannot help you shine your light by talking about your light. I can only help you shine your light by shining mine.

The thread continued on as these things do. Nobody was convinced to change position on the spot (go figure, LOL), but prayerfully all had something to learn, including me. After signing off, however, I couldn't shake the feeling that something was missing, that more needed to be said, and that I didn't articulate all that I could or should have.

This morning, however, I read an article in the January 17, 2012 issue of The New York Daily News that brought the whole conversation home for me.

Read the article here. http://www.nydailynews.com/news/world/bulldog-adopts-wild-boar-piglets-germany-article-1.1024160

At a Berlin animal sanctuary, six wild boar piglets, whose mother had apparently been killed by hunters, were brought in shivering and cold. Instantly, a French Bulldog named Baby, a "veteran" resident, ran over to the piglets and snuggled them all to keep them warm. She has not left their side since. A video shows Baby playing with the piglets, who have clearly taken to her as "Mom." What's even more remarkable is that according to sanctuary worker Norbert Damm, Baby has adopted and raised "raccoons, cats and many other animals."

And there it is. I felt almost ashamed that Baby knows more about love than some people I know. If you think that the love between Baby and those piglets is somehow different or less significant than human love for one another, then I double-dog dare you to try to harm one of those piglets in Baby's presence. She is, after all, a bulldog. And if you know anything about the strength, power and ferocity of a full grown boar, I dare you to harm a hair on Baby's head once those piglets have grown.

While we're arguing over the internet about whether or not one type of human being can love another, and what it might mean for one's sense of identity or self-appreciation if one dares to love a human that is <gasp> different, Baby just lives her life giving love to all creatures who come across her path, irrespective of appearance, species membership, etc., and they're all the healthier and happier for it.

And a French Bulldog named Baby shall lead them.

May we all learn from her example.

REAL TALK WITH REAL MEN: FOR WOMEN ONLY

I had the distinct honor and pleasure of sitting on the distinguished panel for "Real Talk with Real Men: FOR WOMEN ONLY" on Morgan State University's campus. The forum took place on Thursday, October 13th, and was sponsored by BET and the Alpha Gamma chapter of Delta Sigma Theta Sorority, Inc. The format lent itself to an impassioned discussion between the sexes. The all-male panel was asked poignant and thought-provoking questions by moderator Dr. Jeri Dyson and an all-female audience.

The panel, both star-studded and provocative, included: Bishop Derek Triplett, Big Tigger, Darien Dennis, Raheem DeVaughn, Sammie, Tjuan, Khalil and Joe Clair. Given the size of the panel and the tremendous personalities involved (has anyone reading this ever tried to moderate a panel with a really funny comic aboard?), Dr. Dyson did a tremendous job reigning us all in while still letting us "flow." And she did all that while managing to keep us on topic! To say that the panel provided "real talk" with provocative and even controversial ideas would be an understatement. This forum was for mature audiences only!

Speaking of the audience, they were both attentive and engaging. They *really* wanted to know how men think, how we engage in relationships, and why "we" have such a hard time showing respect to our ladies. The panel was not shy in sharing its opinion, and thankfully, we didn't all agree on each point. Our disagreements made for some colorful conversation. For my part, I couldn't keep the old educator in me from showing up, and I made a point of framing our relationships and much of the conversation in a historical context.

A huge kudos goes out to Vikki Kennedy Johnson, BET's Manager of Public Affairs for the forum series "Rap It Up." She coordinated the event and her organizational skills were clearly evident, as it all went off without a hitch. Thank you Vikki for inviting me!

I also want to say thank you to Dr. Dyson, to the panel for allowing me to share their space, and last but not least, THANK YOU to the audience! They were all fantastic.

Watch out for pics and video clips to be posted to steveberlack.org shortly! You'll be sure to catch the "flavor" of the discussion! What do *you* have to say about all this?

CRAZY & DERANGED - WHY DO WE IGNORE THE SIGNS? CAFFEINE WITH F.J. CARTER

I had the pleasure yesterday afternoon (10.2.11) of being a guest on the BlogTalk Radio Show Caffeine with F. J. Carter. The show was entitled: "Trigger Happy 2 - Crazy and Deranged - Why Do We Ignore The Signs?" Along with fellow guests Kenda Bell and Marlena Ann Russell, we discussed the nature of relationships, what makes them go off "the deep end," and whether or not we can see the signs of a crazy mate before the relationship gets serious.

Listen to the archived show here. http://www.blogtalkradio.com/majestic-pen/2011/10/02/trigger-happy-iicrazy-derangedwhy-do-we-ignore-the-signs

It was a great conversation, as the topics ranged from ways in which significant others manifest their "craziness," the impact of our relationships with parents on our romantic relationships, self-awareness, communication issues and the impact of breakdowns in communication, domestic violence and more. Although the hostess and guests continuously shared their wisdom on these subjects, the highlight of the show, for me, came when a caller shared her story.

The caller courageously spoke about being raped at a very young age, and then experiencing this violence again in life. She also noted that these traumas have impacted her in that she now tends to look for men in relationships that she knows are not good for her. We were all inspired when she claimed her victory there on the show by letting us know that she would fight the demons brought on by her trauma and move on to a positive life and impact on others. We all applauded her courage and let her know that it is exactly that kind of determination and willingness to help others by sharing that makes her a survivor, and not a victim, as Kenda Bell so eloquently stated.

The show essentially ended when each guest gave their advice on how to approach new relationships so as to avoid the "crazy and deranged" potential mates out there. Here was my advice:

1) You don't need a relationship to be happy. Find your happiness within so that you may truly share that happiness with another.

2) Know yourself! You must come into a relationship knowing which issues are negotiable for you, and which are not.

3) Do *not* compromise what is not negotiable.

4) Communicate what you've discovered to any potential mate.

5) If you see signs that your potential mate is "crazy and deranged," *act* immediately. Rule number one: if someone shows you who s/he is, believe him or her the *first* time.

6) If the relationship ever - even once - turns violent or threatens to, seek professional help immediately. Do not try to figure it out on your own,

and do not take on the responsibility of "changing" him or her. That's your mate's job, and s/he may not want it.

I'd like to thank the hostess F.J. Carter for having me aboard, the other guests, and the callers and listeners who made it such a dynamic show. Keep up the great work, and let's keep talking, and keep healing.

WHAT GOOD MEN LOOK LIKE

I spent the past weekend participating in a men's conference at New Psalmist Baptist Church in Baltimore.

As a member, I was proud to hear Bishop Walter Thomas, Sr., Pastor of New Psalmist, announce that there were over one thousand men registered and engaged in an event designed to bring men together in peace, love and testimony. **Over one thousand.** From Friday evening, through all-day workshops on Saturday, to the concluding service on Sunday, we learned about walking in faith, men as leaders in our families, our communities and our church, and what sacrifices we must make to live in the expectation of blessings to come.

At various intervals, and in small groups throughout the church, we held hands, stood in circles and bowed our heads, praying together, giving testimony and acknowledging our submission to God. We hugged, laughed, told each other we loved and respected one another, and shared stories. As I walked along the lower levels of the church, heading towards another workshop, I saw such a circle in a small, private conference room off to the side. The thought struck me: this is what good men look like. I remembered the many conversations I've had with people who've told me that such a thing as good men don't exist. They claim that we're not here. Present. Alive. Making a difference.... They say that they themselves have never seen a good man.

And so to them I say this: one doesn't have to be a member of New Psalmist to be a good man. One doesn't have to join our particular prayer circles. One didn't have to attend the conference. But if the conference confirmed anything, it's that **there are good men out there.** And we're not afraid to proclaim both our submission to something greater than us, and to proclaim our subsequent greatness.

Leaders. Fathers. Husbands. Brothers. Uncles. Sons. Nephews. Friends.

And if you don't see us...where are you looking?

RING THE ALARM! MARRIAGE IN THE 21ST CENTURY

I just read a disturbing article in the March 2011 issue of Ebony Magazine entitled "State of Black Marriage." It begins with an anecdote about an African American woman named Cleo Lightfoot who discusses the lack of happy marriages she has seen, and the philosophy her relationships have been rooted in:

"I was taught at an early age that I didn't need a man for anything."

She is a doctoral candidate in clinical psychology. So, is she right? If we're talking about her ability to challenge her intellect, have a fulfilling career, educate herself and be a model for others, she certainly is. But if we're talking about living a fulfilled and happy life, and having a positive social impact on her children and the children around her, then we're getting into some serious gray area.

To demonstrate my point, a 12-year-old African-American male student of the DC Public School System provides a quote in the article that illustrates the damage that such a philosophy has on the psyche and self-perception of impressionable children:

"Marriage is for White people."

Wow. Disturbing. To say the least. Statistics provided by The Pew Study (in conjunction with Time Magazine) quoted in the article speak to the young man's point:

- In 1960, 68% of all "twenty-somethings" were married. In 2008, that was true of just 26%.
- In 1960, 61% of Black adults were married. By 2008, that share had dropped to 32%, compared with 56% of Whites.
- Among Black women giving birth in 2008, 72% were unmarried. **Seventy-two percent!!** This compares with 53% of Hispanic women and 29% of Whites.

Not only has the marriage rate among young adults dropped precipitously amongst all Americans, the marriage rate amongst African-Americans has dropped on a whole different scale. And it's having a negative impact on how our children see themselves and how they view the necessity of marriage and long-term relationships.

By the end of the article, however, we see hope for all Americans. Having undergone a six-month premarital counseling class at her church, Mrs. Cleo Lightfoot-Booker, the same "strong, independent" woman we met at the beginning of the article, notes that seeing real-life examples of what good marriages looked like helped her to learn to trust her mate. She dropped this pearl of wisdom:

"I now believe that marriage is a learning process, (as is) being in a relationship. To learn something, you must be patient, make mistakes and overcome obstacles without giving up."

Amen and amen. Adults: we've got to step our game up. No matter our views on marriage, we've got to see beyond ourselves and consider the impact of our relationship decisions on our children and our neighbors' children. The statistics tell us this is critical. We are (and definitely should be) in emergency mode. Ring the alarm. And let's reconsider where we stand.

THE BETTER ANGELS

I've just recently come to understand that we are all in pain. In some form or another. In some degree or another.

Some of us wear our pain on our sleeves for all to see. Shouting our pain to the hilltops. Uncaring who knows it...who sees it...or who recoils from it. We try to rant our pain away. Push our pain away. We stare people in the eye and tell them if they make one false step, we're gonna.... And little do others know that what we're really saying is: "HELP ME!!"

Some of us absorb our pain. Internalize our pain. Quiet our pain away.... We hold our pain inside, scared for anyone to see it. We hold it in so well that our bodies shake from the exertion of our efforts. The pain creeps out onto our faces, unbeknownst to us. Our eyes catch those of others around us, and without speaking, we plead: "HELP ME!!"

I'm here to tell you that Angels of Pain are all around us. Whether they're shouting to the rooftops or silently pleading with us, they're *near*. They are our mothers, fathers, sisters, brothers, aunts, uncles, friends, and yes... our enemies.

So the next time someone is in your face and passing that pain to you, be The Better Angel. Remember what they're really saying, and give them a warm, heartfelt smile. Let them know you're listening, that what they say matters, and watch what happens to that pain. Instead of jumping into their pit of pain, pull them up to your ledge of light. It may not be comfortable for you. You may not like the feeling. But who said it's about you? Who knows? You might just save a life....

CHAPTER 8

Parenting

"Tell me and I forget, teach me and I may remember, involve me and I learn." — Benjamin Franklin

"Trust yourself. You know more than you think you do." — Benjamin Spock

"Children have never been very good at listening to their elders, but they have never failed to imitate them." — James Baldwin

Author's Notes:

"Parenting: (or child rearing) is the process of promoting and supporting the physical, emotional, social and intellectual development of a child from infancy to adulthood. Parenting refers to the aspects of raising a child aside from the biological relationship." – Wikipedia

I read this definition and was floored. What struck me was the distinction between biological relationships and child rearing. We often assume when we meet "mothers" or "fathers" that they automatically behave in certain ways. We assume they love their children unconditionally. We assume they teach their children right from wrong. We assume they share lessons about family history and treating others as they wish to be treated. My mother, however, told me something quite different when I was a child: "Giving birth does not make one a mother." At first, I had no idea what she was talking about. It wasn't until I became an adult and had children of my own that the wisdom of her words became exceptionally clear. The corollary is true as well: getting someone pregnant does not make one the father.

As a teacher and administrator in a major public school system, I became acutely aware that children mirror their environments. During my first year of teaching, I had one particular student that I couldn't figure out. He was intelligent, gregarious and had the finest clothes. The kids all loved him. However, he seemed unable to refrain from cursing in my classroom and disrupting the class with inappropriate antics. I talked to him about it often, made clear the specific behaviors I expected of him, and let him know that it mattered to me that he succeed in my class. But he wouldn't stop. So I called his mother. And then I understood. Between her screaming in my ear and constantly interrupting our conversation to turn away from the phone and cuss out the kids in the background, (she *did* know I could hear her, right?), it dawned on me that my job would be to help my student unlearn behaviors he brought with him.

I also acutely remember a young lady in my class. She was shy, very quiet and had few friends. She studied diligently, and though she didn't always get A's, she never failed, and I could see that she earned every bit of grade she got. One day I happened upon her father in the hallway, and after he introduced himself, I immediately saw the reflection of him in his little girl. He had the same quiet yet strong and determined look about him. There was pride in his voice when he spoke her name, and there was a sense of respect for the profession of teaching I didn't always see in our parents.

Although how a child is raised isn't the sole indicator of future success, proper parenting buttressed by love and discipline lays a very strong foundation for a child to build upon.

When I had children of my own, I learned something equally important: parenting is as much about learning as it is about teaching. The first thing I learned: parenting gives the great gift of allowing me to live again. When my first daughter was born, things I had learned long ago and had taken for granted became fresh lessons through her eyes. Tori was just a few months old and laying in my arms as we enjoyed a warm, summer day together on the front lawn. I found myself constantly staring at her face, still in awe that she was here, bonding with me every second that she lay safe tucked comfortably in my arms. After a time, however, I noticed that she was not looking at me. She was staring up, not blinking. I looked up as well, (don't we all do that?), and saw nothing more than the familiar tree casting its shadow. I went back to gazing at her. After a few minutes, I realized that she had not shifted her gaze one iota, and seemed transfixed by…something. It dawned on me that she had to see something, so when I looked up to the tree again and saw nothing, I kept staring, like she did. Sure enough, tucked away in the upper branches, well camouflaged from any cursory glance, was a bird's nest. In the nest were three chicks, hungrily stretching their necks upwards and chirping loudly for mommy to feed them. And there was Mama Bird, stoic and purposeful, complying.

I couldn't believe that I had walked past that tree for months and never noticed the nest. And once I realized the chicks were chirping, I couldn't help but hear them from that point on. And I couldn't believe how loud they were! Just like Tori when she was hungry. I re-learned an old and important lesson from Tori that day: stop and look around. Life and all its beauty is happening all around me. If I get too caught up in my own world, I miss the great joys of living.

My youngest daughter, Chrissy, has taught me valuable lessons as well. Just as I did as a child, Chrissy draws all the time. I'm always ready for the familiar "Daddy, look!" as she eagerly places another drawing directly in front of my face. (Raise your hand, parents, if you've had a moment like this, or ten thousand). One day she drew a picture of me, and after giving her congratulations on capturing my likeness so well, I posted the picture on social media to show off. The responses that came back were astounding. I realized that she had not only drawn a picture of me, she told me how she sees me as a dad and as a man. I re-learned another valuable lesson: you are always being watched, and the way you present yourself can have profound implications for the people around you. You can read about it more in "How Children See Us."

Questions For Your Consideration

Following are some questions that may guide you through this chapter:

1) What lessons do you focus on when teaching your children? Why those in particular?
2) What have you learned from your children?
3) Are you a better parent now than you were your first day? Why/not?
4) What can you do better today as a parent to continue your growth?
5) Do you parent children that are not yours biologically? Why/not?

Becoming "Daddy" has made me grow in ways I never thought possible. I've learned *patience*, unconditional love, patience, how to connect between the old and the new, patience, how to re-learn lessons, and…oh yeah… *patience*. Parenting is easily the most difficult and most rewarding job on the planet. I hope this chapter helps you reflect on your parental journey, and I pray that the smile on your face reflects mine as I type this. See you at the Epilogue.

THEY'RE NOT PROMISED

Parenting is the hardest job in the world. Period.

One of the most difficult aspects of parenting is walking the fine line between being your children's confidant, and their disciplinarian. There's a very fine line between going crazy because they keep running up and down the stairs and making a racket, and smiling as they present you with the picture they drew of you when you weren't looking, your heart warming as your face blushes because you were *just* about to get on them for that broken family heirloom....

You beam with pride as your child takes off for the first time on his/her new bike, free and independent. Then you try to make sense of your crazy, mixed emotions as you realize that your children don't like the games/sports/things you did as a kid, and would much rather do (input anything that you loathed at the same age).

Children are every real parent's greatest joy. And every *real* parent's greatest frustration. I say every real parent's frustration because real parents care enough to go through that emotion behind their children's actions. Even if they don't ever want to admit how truly frustrated they are. Children are frustrating because, as their parent, it matters to you when you try to explain something fundamental to their survival and well-being, but they completely ignore your advice/command and do their own thing so that they may experience life for themselves. How many of you know the kid that ignored your warning and burned her hand on the stove because she touched the fire *anyway?*

And then there's the teenage years. It's difficult, to say the least, to give advice to someone who looks like you, lives in your house, and eats your food, while overtly rebelling against everything you hold sacred and dear. How many parents have asked themselves: "Was I *that* bad as a kid?" How many parents have made that phone call to mom and dad because they just have to get confirmation: "Did I really do all that when I was little?" How many parents sat embarrassed and annoyed when Grandma and Grandpa gave out the snickering "I told you so's!"?

And here's the kicker: no matter how old your children grow, no matter how many children they have, and no matter how many children their children have, they will always be your little boys and girls. They will always be your *children*. Though finally wise enough to seek your advice (go figure!) with careers, homes, cars and retirement plans, they're still the little kids you remember riding off on their bikes so many decades ago....

So parents, when you're feeling frustrated, when your child is standing in front of you and telling that flat-out fib: "No Daddy, of *course* I didn't go to the mall, because remember how you told me I couldn't go this week?", just remember one thing. Your children were not promised to you. You could have had any other children. And you could have been any other child's parent.

Remember, you and your children are together for a reason. You're all learning, loving and teaching each other. They are your greatest blessing. And if you need a little private comfort, remember too: if you do your job as a real parent, they are just as frustrated with you.

HOW CHILDREN SEE US

Several days ago, my six year daughter Christina proudly showed me a drawing she had just completed. She used an electronic drawing pad, similar, I thought, to my old Etch-A-Sketch. I'm old...I know. In a refrain heard by parents all over the world, Chrissy proudly exclaimed in her outdoor voice: "Daddy, look what I drew!" She then shoved the electronic drawing doo-hickey in front of me. What I saw on the pad immediately filled me with an exhilarating mix of pride, awe and laughter....

What struck me first was the unusually round and bald head, followed by some rather large glasses, and a dark mass under the chin that looked part goatee/part bow tie. What caused my unusual emotional reaction was the realization that the character was me! There I was, rather remarkably and accurately depicted, in box-man form. Really, it was uncanny how much he *looked* like me. I immediately smiled, yelled out: "Wow! That's me!" and gave Chrissy a big, old bear hug and kiss, followed by a high five. My six year old just stood there, beaming, looking back and forth between Daddy and his doppelganger. Yep, she got me just right!

Of course, being the proud Papa that I am, I took a picture of my twin and posted him on my social media pages. At first, everyone commented on how cute the picture was, but then something interesting occurred. People started noticing not just how much he looked like me, but they made note of how he was drawn.

I have to admit, I didn't really think about it at first. So I looked at the picture again. And yes, sure enough, Daddy Doppelganger looks just as they described him. He has a huge, friendly and warm smile. He stands tall and erect. He is clearly a proud man. His most prominent feature is a large, dark mass under his chin. My first instinct was to identify it as a bow tie, based on my self-perception. But then I remembered, Chrissy always comments on, plays with, and scratches my goatee. She's fascinated by it. To her, my goatee is most prominent feature, because it represents "Daddy." The goatee *is* me.

Lastly, I noticed the wide open arms, held in perfect position to give her the hug that she knew was coming. Like looking at the picture of the young/old woman that constantly shifts one's perception, I no longer saw Daddy Doppelganger, but I saw "Daddy," which is her word for me. And Daddy was saying: "I love you, I'm here for you, and you'll always have my smile, a warm hug, and my protection."

I was floored. I cannot think of a more poignant way to remind me of my responsibility to demonstrate to her what a man is, and what he should represent to her. Comfort. Love. Protection. Warmth. Like the sweet, cherry-scented smoke from Grandpa's pipe that forever wafts through my mind, my goatee, smile and open arms are forever nestled in hers.

FLOORED.

That is how my child sees me. How do your children see you?

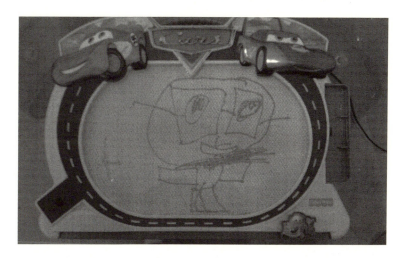

"THE CURRENT" SAYS WE CARE ABOUT AMBER COLE (AND OUR BOYS)

Last night, 10/26/11, I was a guest on the BlogTalkRadio show "The Current," hosted by Kenda Bell. The topic for this show was "I Care About Amber Cole!" and was driven by the video of a 14 year old girl performing fellatio on her ex-boyfriend. This act was performed in front of their school in broad daylight, with at least one other teenaged boy filming it on his phone, and several other boys sitting in plain sight of Amber, watching and laughing. The show was also driven by a thought-provoking article written by my fellow guest, Christelyn Russel-Karazin, a columnist for Madame Noire Magazine. Her article, "Our Apathy: Amber Cole and the Disvaluation of Black Girls," inspired Kenda to put it on The Current's agenda.

See Christelyn's article here. http://madamenoire.com/79202/our-apathy-amber-cole-and-the-disvalue-of-black-girls/

Listen to The Current show archived here. http://www.blogtalkradio.com/kenda-bell/2011/10/27/i-care-about-amber-cole-black-on-black-emotional-hate-crime-1#.TqgzUI_qcnE.facebook

What made the show so poignant was that each of us came at the issue from different perspectives, adding different points to the discussion. While Christelyn and Kenda spoke eloquently about their outrage at the vitriol aimed at Amber for her actions, I pointed out that the "young men" in the video were still stuck at "boy" stage, and that their participation in this horrendous act spoke to the same need for attention and love attributed to Amber. The fact that any of them engaged in this and went so far as to post it on the internet raised some serious red flags about their levels of self-esteem, pride and self-awareness.

A hot topic tossed about the show was the idea that the video and its participants were symptoms of much larger community value issues playing out across the country. Questions and answers (not all agreed upon), were raised concerning who was responsible (parents, schools, the community, etc.), what were the root causes, and how to proceed from here; for us as a community, for this country, and most significantly, for Amber and these nameless boys.

Several guests called in and added tremendously to the conversation. Among the callers were Mia Miata, who spoke about our need for self-evaluation as a community, and PeaJae Cannon, who spoke about the process and need for healing. I should point out that Ms. Cannon and I had a rather hot but respectful debate about the role of historical context in the Amber Cole incident, and whether or not remembering our past means continuing to hold onto pain that stunts our ability to move forward. There were several other callers, and I ask their forgiveness that I do not remember all of their names.

Kudos and a heartfelt thank you to Kenda Bell for hosting the show, to Christelyn for a great article and commentary, and to all of the callers and listeners. So, now that the show is over, *what do we do next?*

A NEW PARENT'S FIRST THOUGHTS: LITTLE SISTER

When my wife and I found out we were expecting our first child, we were both, to say the least, extremely excited. We were overcome with the joy of being selected as instruments to bring forth another life. It was as overwhelming as it was empowering. We talked about everything: what the baby would look like, where the baby would get his or her characteristics, what s/he would become.... When we found out our first baby was a girl, we grew even more excited that we were that much closer to seeing her and understanding who she would be. As a father, knowing that I was about to have a little girl got me thinking.

Could I really handle being a little girl's first love, her male role model? How could I even begin to model for her the blessings I wanted her to have in life? That led me to think: can I handle being her first teacher? As I thought about that, I realized that not only could I handle those things, but being a parent meant that I *must* handle them with care, authority and grace. So, what to teach her?

I figured that the first thing that I as a parent should teach my daughter is who she is. And who could teach her that better than her mother and father? I can remember rubbing my wife's belly as I thought about these things, and, by the grace of God, the poem "Little Sister" came to me as we waited for her to be born. I wrote the poem immediately after talking to my little girl one night in Mommy's belly. The night she came into this world, I held her in my arms and told her the history of her family. I told her who she was. And this poem was waiting for her:

Little Sister

Maya. Toni. Angela. N'tozake. Winnie.
Alice. Shirley. Madame CJ. Cleopatra.
Harriet. Ruth.

African drums. Head ties. Braids.

Chocolate and Cocoa. Butter.
Gazelle-steps in clouds of mother-dust.
Flashing kente.

I-M-A-N-I. Princesse Nubienne.

Hot combs. Sizzling stoves: bacon & grits,
Honey-glazed ham, macaroni & cheese & apple pie
(Always apple pie) – apples picked off the ground
And riding in your apron….

Blazing heat. Sun-burnt curves. Mother-love breasts.
The true heartland, found in mounds.
Musky. Earthy. Life & Love.

The sacrifices of the elders pledge you
To the sisterhood.

Your sorors are calling.
Come out… come out…
Little sister.

That was 10 years ago. We've since had a second beautiful little girl. So we keep teaching. And they keep challenging us to learn.

Anyone reading this who is a parent knows that parenting is the most difficult, frustrating, challenging and utterly beautiful job in the world. So, how do you handle it? Dad, what do you think about when you rub Mom's belly? Mom, what do you wish to pass on to your baby? What do you teach your children? And, just as important: what are you willing to learn?

LEGACY

"There but for the grace of God go I."

I've heard that phrase since I was a child. I understood the words and their definitions when I was young, but it wasn't until I became older and more "seasoned" that I understood what it meant.

I grew up in the South Bronx to a single parent just out of high school and without a father who was killed in Vietnam before he got the chance to meet me. I've often wondered why I didn't wind up stuck on those streets, drinking the same drink and smoking the same "smoke" and talking smack to the same friends on the same corner...year after year...decade after decade. In 1979, a group called Machine came out with a hit song called: "There But For The Grace of God Go I." At 14 years old, I hardly noticed the words as I danced to Machine's beat, and roller-skated my way to joyous nights with friends and family, buoyed by the boogie. The next fall, I said goodbye to all of them as I embarked on my journey to Phillips Academy in Andover, Massachusetts. I was aware that I was attending the number one ranked prep school in the nation, but painfully unaware as to how or why. If you asked me then, I would have told you it was because I was smart. I know now that it was because I was aware of who I was and where I came from.

"There but for the grace of God go I."

Someone asked me once if I talk the way I do because I went to Andover. I replied that I went to Andover because I talk, and *think*, the way I do.

"There but for the grace...."

That journey to Andover re-set the course of my life, as I lived, collected and internalized experiences that would inform The Berlack Method, LLC. When I stand before an audience of folks who look like me, not just physically but emotionally, mentally and spiritually, and who struggle with the same issues that I've encountered, I remember that song and that phrase. And I remember that The Berlack Method, the tool God gave me to speak to my audience, is the legacy of three people, all of whom reside in me:

My grandfather, Weston Berlack, is the model for my manhood training. He was gregarious, funny, extremely charming, handsome and very giving. My first visions of manhood came through him. To this day, whenever I think of him, the smell of cherry tobacco from his ever-present pipe wafts through my mind. He never left the house without wearing a suit and tie. He always wore his fedora. People comment about the fedora I wear with my own suit and tie, because they're not used to seeing someone so young with such an old style. I just smile and think of Grandpa.

When I was very young, I attempted to steal a bag of potato chips from the neighborhood store. My mother whipped me, but I don't remember the whipping. What I remember is my grandfather sitting me down on his bed as he told me, in a very low tone: "Son, it starts with this." He then placed a pencil on the nightstand. "It then becomes this." He placed a book next to the pencil. "Then it will be this." He moved the large lamp next to the book. He then proceeded to tell me about his 29 years as a private detective in New York and his service in a segregated U.S. army in World War II. He regaled me with stories about his son, Albert Berlack, who was a Court Officer at the time. Maintaining his low tone, he then said something I never forgot: "We've always been on the right side of the law." As he pointed to the items on the nightstand, he said: "Berlacks don't do that," then turned on his heel and left the room. I never did anything close to breaking the law since, and if any Berlack Method audience member sees pride and dignity in me, this is in large part where it comes from. Grandpa taught me how to be a man. He also taught me what it means to be a Berlack.

My grandmother, Elise Berlack, also resides in me and in The Berlack Method. Sunday morning meant going to church with Grandma. Sunday afternoon meant getting stuffed by a huge "supper" that she prepared: ham, turkey, chicken, macaroni and cheese, greens, rice and peas, the works. And of course, there was always the fresh apple/sweet potato/lemon meringue pie that she baked from scratch the day before. How good a cook was she? Her food tasted like she loved us. The entire family knew without question where to spend every holiday.

She was the most loving, giving and kind person I've ever known. She spoiled me when my mother would not. She was an old-fashioned Southern woman: pious and hospitable to a fault. She always had a hot meal, a warm smile, a big hug and a ready ear waiting for me whenever I visited. She taught me how to love.

"There but for...."

My mother, Delores Berlack, also resides in me. She was stern and demanding. She was the type of mom that stood with me as I did my homework, and reviewed my class notes. When I got a good grade from my teacher, she would go over my work with a red pen, and demanded that I finish it again to her satisfaction. When I spoke, "dis" had to become "this." "Dose" had to become "those." I hated doing my homework around her, but I thank her to this day.

She provided me with everything I ever needed. She put a roof over my head and clothes on my back, almost entirely by herself. I used to complain that she always bought me "Skippies" instead of "Pro Keds," but today, I'm grateful that the pavement never touched my feet.

"There...."

When I stand before my audience as President of The Berlack Method, I often find myself saying: "My mother told me…" or "my mother taught me…." She taught me perseverance and to demand more of myself than anyone else could. She taught me the tough love and discipline I pass on to all who hear me speak.

Here's to you, Grandma, Grandpa and Ma. There is no Berlack Method without you. There but for the grace of God go I.

JANKS MORTON DOES IT AGAIN

I recently had the privilege of attending the Montgomery County, Maryland screening of the Janks Morton documentary: *Guilty Until Proven Innocent*. The film proved to be a powerful illuminator of the tremendous and untold strife, despair and torturous circumstances faced by fathers in the Family Court and Child Support systems.

Gritty and raw, the documentary features interviews by Producer/Director Janks Morton, who sits with several fathers as they recount the horror stories they've faced when former spouses used both their anger and their children to punish them. Each story is as heart-wrenching as the next, and, sitting in the audience, I could feel the tension rising until one father, completely overwhelmed, succumbed to his emotions in front of the camera, unable to stop himself.

As someone who has worked closely with several fatherhood groups, I am all too clear that these stories are being repeated across the nation. Unfortunately, the plight of these fathers are not only hidden by the national media, they are made more horrific by the cold-as-steel dismissal of these fathers by the systems charged with guarding "the best interests of the children."

Speaking of the children, Mr. Morton provided great insight into the vast scope of divorce and the state of our community family structures by interviewing several youth during the film. He asked them to say their names and reply to the question: "Are your parents married, divorced, separated or never married?" It was appalling to find that *not one* youth lived in a home with married parents. Although only a small sample was provided, it was a grim reminder of the terrible scale of the breakdown of the American family structure. Most of the youth remarked as well that a child of divorce should unequivocally be placed with the mother.

These interviews give us insight into why the plight of fathers generally, and Black males in particular, with the exception of other works by Morton himself, such as *Men II Boys,* are literally ignored by the general public. This ignorance must end. No matter what side of the Child Support fence one might find oneself, how can we effectively provide the best for our children by ignoring the injustices endured by any of their parents?

A brief panel discussion was held after the viewing by stakeholders in the Maryland area. Maryland Delegate Jill Carter, one of the panelists that was featured in the film, remarked on the severity of the injustices fathers face on various socio-political levels. She sponsored a bill in the House of Delegates that called for a reform of the system that determines percentage of custody time between mother and father. Her bill included some ideas deemed radical by the establishment, including a call to end the exchange of money between parents when they both have equal custody. According to Delegate Carter, the Women's Caucus of the House walked out of the building, and refused to even debate the issue. As she stated during the panel discussion: "If you're so convinced about the validity of your position, why be afraid to debate it?"

Hear, hear....

The following is an excerpt from the film description provided on the DVD:

For decades, sociologists, psychologists and academics have examined the plethora of social ills children of divorce encounter over their lifetimes. For the first time, the fathers of divorce are given a platform and a voice to share their most intimate feelings around the challenges of not having full and complete access to their children. We all have

heard the stories of biased family courts, bitter spousal retributions, exorbitant alimony, child-support and lawyer fees, but have we ever stopped to wonder what goes on in the heart of a father, when he is alone, with no knowledge of where his children are?

Guilty Until Proven Innocent features Dr. Linda Nielsen, Maryland Delegate Jill Carter, Michael McCormick, Kenneth Williams and Hans Olsen. It is a must see. Please visit www.whatblackmenthink.com to find out more about this documentary and other projects by Janks Morton.

Thank you Mr. Morton, and all involved, for all you do to bring light to a dark and persistently challenging issue.

What are your thoughts on this?

DONUTS FOR DADS

I had the honor of addressing the dads of Pimlico Elementary/Middle #223 at their annual Donuts for Dads event. Rev. Al Bailey of New Psalmist Baptist Church also spoke. Of course, supplying coffee and donuts is a great way to gather dads, (at least for me it is), and the Senior Lounge provided a nice, relaxed atmosphere for our discussions.

Rev. Bailey discussed the many resources at hand at New Psalmist, and about the recent Men's Conference. I gave a brief speech about the difference between father and dad, using my own life as an example. I loved the fact that many of the dads pulled their kids from classrooms to be present at the discussion, and things got very interesting when Ms. Peterson, the coordinator of the event, left the room so that we could have real, live talk in our "man cave."

We discussed the things men want to talk about, and I was delighted to see that all of the dads participated, giving each other advice and encouragement. I provided a little guidance here and there, but the men really took over and took leadership of the event. It really warmed my heart to see it.

The feedback we received from the dads was that they wanted to have more time to connect and communicate with each other, and that they wanted to do this kind of event more often. We will do our best to comply. These dads deserve it. Kudos to Jackie Peterson, Elneeta Jones, Principal of Pimlico and Rev. Al Bailey for making this event happen.

This is the kind of story that should be in the news! What do you think?

PARENT UP!!! IT'S THAT SERIOUS

By all accounts, last night's community open forum: "Parent Up!! Who's Parenting Who?" was a great success. I was proud to co-present the event with Caprice Smith, President of SharperMinds Consultants. Thank you and kudos to the co-hosts: Pimlico Elementary/Middle School #223, Ms. Elneeta Jones, Principal, (with a special thanks to Jackie Peterson and Wanda Williams), Park Heights Renaissance, Inc., the wonderful panel: Bonita Linkins, Felicia Roach, Lisa Calicchia and Duane Williams, and an informed and participative audience.

There was much to discuss, and a lot of great points of interest, stories, information, support and concerns passed around the room. It seemed that just as passions were getting at their highest, it was time to end the forum. Principal Jones made an impassioned plea for parental involvement and assistance at Pimlico and throughout the system. That is why it was especially important that several members of the audience took it upon themselves to exchange contact information with a promise to meet further on the issue of parenting and to *take action!!* We were especially pleased to see contact information exchanged, as that is the very point of the forum series.

Given all that, I believe that it is not coincidence that on the same day of the forum, a story was printed in the New York Daily News about a 16 year-old boy that beat his mother to death with a hammer because she took away his PlayStation after an argument.

See the article here. http://www.nydailynews.com/news/national/kendall-anderson-16-killed-mom-claw-hammer-playstation-court-article-1.139414

When a mother is murdered in cold blood (according to the article, he confessed to mulling over what to do for hours before bludgeoning her), by her own son after he was disciplined by her, we are given a stark reminder that this issue is *that serious.*

We've got work to do. And if we don't do it, who will? Time to roll those sleeves up....

THE POWER OF A CHILD'S UNCONDITIONAL LOVE

There's something about the power of a child's love. It is blind, faithful, unyielding, and best of all: unconditional. Any parent who looks into his/her child's eyes can see it. It is overwhelming and absolutely humbling to know that despite your faults and missteps, your child still loves you, and still needs you.

Nowhere is this more apparent than in the case of Ms. Wanda Rodriguez, a nurse at a Bronx hospice who checked in on her new patient recently. His name was Victor Peralta, and she quickly realized that this was her estranged father, whom she had not seen in 41 years. She broke into tears when he acknowledged that he had two grown daughters, Gina and Wanda. I can't imagine the feelings she experienced at that admission. Surely she had to have feelings of anger, frustration, wonderment, awe (what are the chances that he would wind up at the hospice where she worked -- after 41 years?), and perhaps, pure joy.

Out of the sheer power of love, father and daughter have continued to strengthen their bond by "cherishing every moment they have left together."

Every parent I've talked to has experienced similar moments with his/her child. The case of Ms. Rodriguez and her father is extreme, to be sure, but all parents fail their children in one way or another. As human beings, we all fall short of a real parent's goal: to provide nothing but the best for our children, and to give them lives that exceed our own in every way. We mess up, we screw up, we forget promises, we get too busy and we work too hard. Our children still love us, and jump into our beds in the morning and want to play with us. I'll never forget the story of Ms. Rodriguez and her dad. And now, I'm going to go play with my own daughters. I'll be back....

NEVER GIVE UP ON OUR CHILDREN

As a personal development expert that facilitates male youth workshops, I'd love to tell you that I always have the answers to every challenge presented to me by my charges. Any of you who are parents would know that it would be pure malarkey if I told you that I did. For me, the biggest difference between training adults and children is that children often don't participate in my workshops of their own accord. Because of this, and because children think differently than adults, when facilitating youth workshops I often have to spend a lot time in the beginning finding the *key* to my audience. I have to find what makes them *tick*, what grabs their attention.

With some groups, I find the key relatively easily. Some groups are naturally trusting and chatty, and I find out quickly that we connect based on things such as a love of sports, movies, music, fashion, etc. Once I find the key, I use it to build my relationship with them, and then hone in on the theme of the workshop to get them to grow.

Some youth groups are far from cooperative, to say the least. In the public school systems I've worked in, I've encountered groups that were downright hostile. I currently facilitate male youth training for such a group in Baltimore. There are three young men in particular who have been disruptive for weeks, and they've done so to a degree I've never encountered before. They fight, yell out, perform inappropriate dances at completely inappropriate times, throw chairs, etc. Now, before you sit there judging me, let me tell you that I've observed this behavior of theirs with everyone at their school, including their teachers and administrators.

And so, as I walked in the door earlier this week, I found myself at wit's end. I was drained. And I found myself in the unfamiliar position of feeling like I'd been…finally…whipped. And whipped bad. The week prior, I decided to make an adjustment in planning and bring my chess set. I also had a movie about chess and the life skills that can be gleaned from the game. I was, however, not optimistic about the chances of my young men actually sitting still for a movie and showing interest in something "boring" like chess.

Then it happened. I opened up my tournament chess bag and set up the game on the middle table. While I set up my laptop, I noticed something strange. There was no noise. No chairs flying. No cursing. No fighting. All of the young men gathered quickly around the board, and then I saw it. The lights in their eyes, burning brightly. Wheels turning upstairs, smiles on their faces.

Not only did they sit through the movie clips and wait patiently as I explained the game to those who were unfamiliar to it, but the one who had given me the most behavioral challenges kept everyone quiet and attentive. Then we played. And he gave me the game of my life. This newly-minted teen promptly engaged me in a wide-open game, defending my attacks deftly and picking apart my defense. With time running out, we declared a draw, but in my secret heart of hearts, (and I suspect in his), I knew he would have won.

Who knew?? It turns out this young man has been playing chess since he was six years old. Most of the young men have played for years as well, which led me to ask Mr. Behavior a question that hadn't occurred to me before: "If you can think three or four moves in advance, and study both your options and your consequences *before* making moves, why do you let the other boys here play you out of position? Why do you behave the way you do in class?" His answer? "I don't know. Sometimes I just get mad."

And there it is. Having found their key, I can now talk to these young men on a completely different level, and with a genuine respect for and bond with one another, because of a game we all love. They can't hide it from me anymore. I've seen it, that light in their eyes, their minds *at work*. I see their intelligence and their wit. All the while I thought I would teach them a thing or two. But in the end, they're the ones who taught me.

Never give up on our children.

Stay tuned. I'm tightening up my game.

OUR ANGRY TEENAGERS ARE GOING WILD

I read a newspaper article in the New York Daily News about a 17 year-old girl in The Bronx who beat a 48 year-old female bus driver. Why? Because the driver, following Metropolitan Transportation Authority policy, wouldn't allow young Steangeli Medina on the bus with her dog unless it was in a crate. How did Steangeli react to this? According to a witness:

She punched the driver in the face. She then drag(ged) her off the bus by her hair ... where she punched and kicked her repeatedly about the body.

The result? The driver was taken to the hospital with a black eye and facial cuts.

See full article here. http://www.nydailynews.com/news/crime/17-year-old-girl-faces-rap-vicious-beatdown-bronx-bus-driver-article-1.128225

There is so much wrong with this story I hardly know where to begin. I'll start with her name.

I'd never heard the name "Steangeli" before, so I looked it up. The first thing the search engine asked me was: "Did you mean to look for "strangely?" I shook my head. The next thing I noticed: there were no definitions of the name available. All that was available were links to the same story about her viciously beating an elder. So, what's the definition of "Steangeli" now? The reason why I searched for a definition is because I strongly believe that naming a child imbues that child with a spirit befitting the name. If you don't know what your name means, and if it really doesn't mean anything, then who are you? Without meaning to rest upon, Steangeli's actions have imbued her name with its own spirit: "I beat my elders." No wonder she's angry. My name? It means "crowned one." I try to live up to that every day.

As a word of advice: if you have a name that has no history or meaning, then it's up to you give spirit to it through your actions. You have the power to define your name. Relish the opportunity and the blessing. If your name does have meaning, live up to it!

Another thing that bothered me was this simple thought: had the bus driver been a man, would she have been bold enough to put her hands on him? I think not. People inherently know who to mess with, and who not to.

The second huge issue here is a blatant lack of respect for one's elders. I don't know anything about Steangeli or how she was raised, so I can't comment on it, except to say that her actions are a direct reflection of her family and her community. My first impression: her parents/elders are clearly having issues with raising her. Perhaps I'm being harsh, but I don't think so. To wit:

When I was a U.S. History teacher at a high school in Baltimore, I drove to work one morning listening to the radio. The story I heard as I pulled up to the school was about a teenaged boy who beat his teacher the day before in another state. Apparently the teacher insisted that the boy stop listening to his MP3 player in the middle of class, and when the student refused, the teacher enforced school rules and confiscated the player. The student promptly beat the much older teacher and hospitalized him.

I decided to put off my lesson plan for a few moments during each class and do some *real* educating. I told my students about the story and asked them: who do you think was right? Almost unanimously, my students replied: "It was the teacher's fault. He shouldn't have taken the player!" So, after hearing this, I closed the door to my classroom, and I had a heart-to-heart with every student I taught that day. I told them simply this: "I love each and every one of you. You are *mine*. So if anyone wants to mess with you, they have to get through me first. But let me tell you one thing. If any of you ever put your hands on me, I'll beat you until I can't find you anymore. Period." And guess what? Outside of the usual crazy teenager stuff, I never had a problem with any of my students. It's called parenting. Tough Love 101. Learn it. Teach it. Live it.

Our angry teenagers are going wild. But, uh…hello? They're teenagers! Part of the definition of "teenager" should be "wild." However, when they cross the line and not only disrespect their elders but hospitalize them, we as the village parents must step forward and take the responsibility charged to us by our age and place in the community. We must do that even if it means letting them know that an @$$-whipping can surely come back their way. That's my take on it, what's yours?

FROM DUBOIS TO THE PREP SCHOOL NEGRO

On the website "Documenting the American South," *The Souls of Black Folk* is described thus:

"W. E. B. Du Bois' *The Souls of Black Folk* (1903) is a seminal work in African American literature and an American classic. In this work Du Bois proposes that 'the problem of the Twentieth Century is the problem of the color-line.' His concepts of life behind the veil of race and the resulting 'double-consciousness, this sense of always looking at one's self through the eyes of others,' have become touchstones for thinking about race in America. In addition to these enduring concepts, *Souls* offers an assessment of the progress of the race, the obstacles to that progress, and the possibilities for future progress as the nation entered the twentieth century."

See the full summary here. http://docsouth.unc.edu/church/duboissouls/summary.html

Given that the publication of DuBois' seminal work on the American questions of race and self-identity occurred in 1903, it must be surprising to some that a documentary entitled *The Prep School Negro* could resonate so resoundingly on the same themes over a century later. This documentary film, produced and directed by André Robert Lee, a 1980's graduate of the prestigious Germantown Friends School in Philadelphia, continues the theme of the inherent tension within (Negroes/Afro-Americans/African-Americans/Blacks - the apropos term has changed much since DuBois) concerning their dual identities of being both Black and American.

See trailer here for a powerful example of this inherent tension. http://www.theprepschoolnegro.org/

As a native of the South Bronx, and as a 1980's graduate of Phillips Academy (Andover), I have felt that tension, as have countless others who hail from inner-city streets and who've been educated on old, blue-blood campuses. I therefore applaud Mr. Lee for continuing discussion on a topic that has not seen nearly enough light. The topic: Who am I as an American? Where do I fit in in an America bold enough to elect its first Black President, yet scared enough to insist on seeing his birth certificate so that he may prove his American roots? What does it mean to go to a prestigious school that sees you as Black, then return home to "friends" who now claim you're no longer "Black enough?"

Being a teenager is hard enough on one's sense of self. Being a Prep School Negro in the shadow of DuBois, now that's something else....

Who are you? And where do you fit in?

PUBLIC SCHOOL ADMINISTRATORS ARE SCARED. PERIOD.

I just finished watching "Your Bottom Line" on CNN, hosted by Christine Romans. The topic of the day was "Fixing the Education System." To say that the problems facing the public education system in America are complex and far-reaching would be an understatement, at best. I was therefore appalled at the simplistic, finger-pointing responses uttered by some of her guests on the show.

As a former educator in a major public school system, (I have experience as a high school history teacher and as an administrator), I have seen first-hand the myriad issues that impact education in general, and what happens within the walls of a classroom in particular. I know that teacher quality (both in terms of certification and pedagogy) has a tremendous impact on the educational progress of students. But I would be remiss if I didn't also note that what happens in the homes and communities of our students is at least as important as anything going on in classrooms! In fact, I would argue that that what happens in homes and communities impact the educational preparation of our students in the first place. But I digress.

On the show, a CNN "Education Correspondent" stated point-blank: "Unions are bad for education." How simplistic can an intelligent man get? How short-sighted can a hard-working, dedicated educator be? He lost me right there. If anyone actually believes that public education (and teachers in particular) would be better off without unions, then consider why unions came to exist in the first place. (For a helpful start: research "The Triangle Shirtwaist Factory Fire." Sorry, that's just the educator in me). If he had said that unions are a necessary evil, and that the interests of the unions sometimes counter what's in the best interests of children, then I would have understood him completely, and would have agreed. Increasing tenure qualification for teachers, paying higher salaries based on merit rather than time on the job, and getting rid of the "last in, first out" policy are all valid arguments. But those ideas are only part of the big picture, and touting them as the be-all, end-all solutions to fixing our public school systems is...well, let me put it point-blank: ridiculous.

Let's not even get started on the fraudulent notion that standardized testing can accurately and fairly demonstrate the effectiveness of teachers. (There's not enough room here to talk about unequal access to resources and information, schools cheating on standardized tests to make themselves look good and protect staff jobs, students passing classes but failing the standardized tests corresponding to those classes, etc.).

So why would a CNN "Education Consultant," a clearly intelligent man who's passionate about children and education, say something as mind-numbingly simplistic as "unions are bad for education?" Because in my experience, administrators are, as a rule, scared of facing all of the issues impacting our children. Administrators would rather fight the battles they feel they can control and win, i.e.: demonizing the teachers they employ, rather than face the far more daunting challenge of *holding parents and their communities responsible* for student preparation, student dedication and work ethic, discipline, educational morale and fundamental principles like respect for elders, all of which have at least an equally important impact on student achievement than test scores.

These administrators are scared because they know that in the environment of "No Child Left Behind," test scores are easier to manipulate and become an easier "win" than changing the attitudes of our students' first teachers: their parents. Administrators know that if they claim parent accountability as an issue, then they stand to have fingers pointed at them when they can't do anything about it. They then face the prospect of being tagged as ineffective elements of education. And why jeopardize their large salaries by taking on a battle they feel they can't win, when they can much more easily blame teacher unions and "the bottom five percent" of teachers? (And somebody, please tell me an industry that doesn't have a "bottom five percent" of its labor force, or that couldn't operate more efficiently by increasing the productivity of said group)?

As a parent, if either of my daughters is not doing well in school, *I see that as my responsibility!!* The first thing I think is: what must I do as their father to ensure their success in school? I believe that that is my responsibility at every level of their educational experience. Their teachers are my partners in this, nothing more or less, and if I ask a teacher to care about my children's education more than I do, then I *know* I'm doing something wrong.

I'd like to point out that the host, Christine Romans, did a great job of moderating such a tough, complicated discussion. However, a conversation about fixing the public school system that doesn't fully address parent and community accountability, and that doesn't feature someone espousing that idea is at best incomplete.

CHAPTER 9

Leadership Development

"A genuine leader is not a searcher for consensus but a molder of consensus." – Martin Luther King, Jr.

"Leadership is the art of getting someone else to do something you want done because he wants to do it." – Dwight D. Eisenhower

"If your actions inspire others to dream more, learn more, do more and become more, you are a leader." – John Quincy Adams

Author's Notes:

"Leadership has been described as 'a process of social influence in which one person can enlist the aid and support of others in the accomplishment of a common task.'" – Wikipedia

The term leadership is very difficult to define fully because as a concept it is very layered, complicated and nuanced. For instance, reading the definition above, the first question that comes to mind for me is: "how exactly does one do all of that?" When I consider all of the people that a leader must influence, including all of their various world views, agendas, wants, needs and motivations, binding them all under one purpose seems impossible. Finding common goals to help unite different people is a start, but how does one know the goals of each person being led, particularly if they are being less than honest? Although there have been many studies that have delineated characteristics that effective leaders share and actions that leaders must take, I submit that one cannot read these studies and become a leader. Leadership is much more art than science.

And there it is. Dwight D. Eisenhower's quote about leadership hit me right between the eyes. Leadership is about *influence* and not about one's title. Influence is a matter of communication (including effective articulation and active listening), sympathy, empathy and action. Leadership is influence in full manifest. And for each person being led, each group being led, and within each geographic area in which leadership is wielded, the style and method of leadership will change, even when the leader is the same. Leadership is art on its own canvas.

One of the greatest misconceptions I've come across about leadership is the idea that influence and power are the same. They are not. Leadership is to influence as one's job or social title is to power. Though they can go hand in hand, one is not necessary to the other. The difference is subtle, which is why I believe so many people get promoted to grandiose titles but can't figure out why nobody is following them. It's also, in my opinion, why so much money is spent on leadership workshops and academies for middle and upper managers and administrators. President Eisenhower captured it perfectly. While a C.E.O. may command someone to do something and get short-term results, a leader *influences* someone to do something and gets long-term, organization-changing results. The reason a leader gets long-term results is because those influenced have bought in to the leader's agenda, claimed it for themselves, and now live and work that agenda on a continuing basis.

As a member of the U.S. Army, I witnessed soldiers who found out about the difference between rank and leadership first hand. Several of my friends, upon promotion to non-commissioned officer status, struggled mightily with the process of leading other soldiers they considered friends. Their common mistake was to "lean on the stripes." When soldiers were slow to obey a command, or when they ignored it altogether, the new "leaders" would often say things like: "that's an order" or "as the squad leader I'm ordering…." Lesson number one: if you have to announce your position in order to get people to do things, you are *not* a leader. You are instead relying on the power vested in your position to get things done. Even if you press that power and get people to move, rest assured they will ignore your next order until you press your authority upon them again. The newly minted Sergeants I knew learned this lesson the hard way, until they realized that they had to engage their charges in open conversation, learn what made them tick, adjust their approach, and re-initiate their leadership of the group. I watched, learned and applied those lessons when I was promoted to Sergeant.

I saw the power of leadership as well as a new employee of a non-profit job readiness training program. We implemented a training program that was very hands-on and confrontational, with a focus on soft skills development. It meant facilitating a lot of "tough love" to adult men and women who were not always used to such treatment. A couple of months after I began, a program participant complained about me to my Executive Director. The ED called me into his office. I remember being very nervous as I entered, and thinking "oh boy, here we go" as he asked me to explain to him what happened. After I fumbled through the story, he asked me to explain, point by point, why I made the decisions that I did. Given that I barely knew the Director, and that this was my first real conversation with him, my initial thought was "dang, I'm about to get fired" as I watched him mull over my explanation in his mind. He then leaned forward in his chair, looked me in the eye, and said: "I understand why you did what you did. As long as you can explain to me why you decide to do something, I'll always have your back. If I disagree with you, I'll tell you privately, and nobody else will know. In fact, given what we do here and how we do it, I would be worried about you if nobody complained." I was stunned by the wisdom of what he said, and felt completely empowered. At that moment, I would have followed him anywhere.

The Blogs

I thought about the above examples when writing "The Cardinal Rule of Leadership." For this particular piece, I wanted to sum up all that I had learned about leadership in one post. I thought about it for a long time. I thought about the elements of leadership, various leadership styles, the distinction between authority and leadership, famous leaders that many admire and what they have in common. In the end, one word kept coming up: servant. The blog explains what I mean.

"Leadership Development Through Opportunity" focuses more on how one develops leadership skills in others. I used examples from my life to pass on what I've learned. One of the themes of this post is that we often find ourselves developing others in ways we did not plan. For instance, when I founded The Berlack Method, I had no idea that within a few years, my sister, her friend (whom I'd never met in person) and a close friend I hadn't seen in years would bond together to create and administer the social media page that drives home messages inherent in The Berlack Method workshops. Though I may be the driving force behind the parent organization, The Berlack Method Group is its own entity that reaches out to over a thousand people on a daily basis, bonding them and uniting them in ways I never considered. People who were connected to various points of my life came together in a way I never anticipated, and though I wield no power or authority over them, they often point out the opportunity afforded them to do something they love – help others, and claim me as the "leader." I submit that I am just the servant, and that they truly are leaders who took on responsibilities without anyone directing them to. That wasn't the plan, but that *is* leadership development.

Questions to Consider

Here are some questions you may wish to consider as you read this chapter:

1. Are you a leader? If so, what makes you one?
2. What is your leadership style? (How do you lead)?
3. Who is your leader?
4. Can you lead without following someone else? Why/not?
5. Who do you lead?
6. Do you choose who you lead, or are your charges "given" to you?
    a. Does that make a difference in how you lead them?
7. Can someone be a leader if s/he is not trained in leadership?

Prayerfully, these questions and the blogs combined will challenge you to meaningful introspection regarding your skills. I submit to you that anyone can be a leader, but most people are decidedly not. Which are you, leader or follower? Be honest. And also consider, how does your answer impact what you believe concerning the other chapters? The answers are designed in The Berlack Method to point you to the final chapter: Community Impact. But we'll get there later. Until then, enjoy the Leadership Development blogs.

See you at the Epilogue.

THE CARDINAL RULE OF LEADERSHIP

If you've ever been part of an organization, then I'd surmise that you must have at some point thought about leadership. Every group has at least one. Given that, my experience has been that more often than not, a huge difference between successful organizations and those that are not so successful is the relative effectiveness of their leadership team.

So what makes leaders effective? What makes them successful? If you do even a cursory online search on leadership, you'll find thousands of articles written about it. Given that leadership has been questioned, examined, written about, and taught in seminars and colleges for centuries, why are there still ineffective leaders?

I'll start the answer by demonstrating what I've seen. In the Army, I often knew soldiers who at some point in their careers were promoted to Sergeant, which marks the transition from worker bee to leader. (Unless, of course, one is in the infantry, etc. in which the rank of Corporal marks the transition, but I digress). The people I knew who were ineffective as new Sergeants immediately changed their relationship dynamics with the soldiers with whom they came into service. They became haughty, and saw their new rank as their most important identifier. I knew some that even looked down their noses socially and professionally at their old friends. These new "leaders" could not understand why soldiers wouldn't ask "how high?" when told to jump, and would bark incessantly and point at the stripes on their uniforms as proof of their authority. Soldiers, in turn, would either stare at them blankly before ignoring the order, or do the exact minimum required to keep from getting barked at any more.

I've seen "leaders" in other organizations that exhibited similar traits. For many of them, the huge degree displayed on the wall was more an indicator of leadership than anything they said or did. Or perhaps the title on their business cards were the thing. And sure enough, when their bosses would question why the organization wasn't operating proficiently, they would blame any and every one under their command.

I've also seen "leaders" reject any idea that wasn't their own. Or, similarly, they would usurp any good idea from their team and portray it as their own when presenting it to the upper echelons of the organization. If you've ever experienced this as a worker, please insert your thoughts/feelings about the individual (here).

Now that I've talked to you about what inhibits leaders from being effective, let me throw out a few names of those that most of us, if not all, acknowledge as leaders and admire. Dr. Martin Luther King, Jr. George Washington. Abraham Lincoln. Sitting Bull. Elizabeth Cady Stanton. Mahatma Gandi. What is it about these leaders that made them so effective? Was it their oratory skills? Their charm? Their intelligence? Their ability to handle pressure and stress? Their ability to connect to and empathize with others?

I submit to you that all of the above are essential elements of leadership. All of the above leaders, and any others one might mention, share most, if not all of those qualities. So what makes a leader a leader? What sets truly effective, life-altering, organization-shifting leaders apart? They've all figured out the cardinal rule of leadership. And if you've ever been a leader, or ever hope to become one, I say to you now that you must not only figure it out as well, but you must absorb it, ponder it and live it as long as you are a leader.

True leaders are *servants* of the people they lead. As simple as that sounds, and as often as you may have already heard that, the reason why there are still ineffective leaders out there is because they don't live it. To be a servant, you must be humble. You must put your ego aside, and realize that the success of the organization or of the people is not about *you*. It's about them. Your leadership ability is in no way tied to your title. In fact, nine out of ten people you work with couldn't care less about your title.

They want to know that you care about them. They want to know that if they need anything from you, they can come to you either in private or in a group and feel no fear of belittlement. They want to feel wanted and needed within the organization. They want to see you pick up the mop and clean the spill by the counter before someone gets hurt. They want to know that they can count on you. They want to know that you hear them when they speak, even if you ultimately don't agree, and decide to do something else.

In introductory business or leadership courses, a distinction is made between authoritative figures and *de facto* leaders (literally meaning leaders "in fact" who have assumed authority irrespective of title or organizational power). Anyone can climb an organization's ladder. Anyone can be "the boss." But only a select few can be leaders, and no business cards are necessary to find them.

If you ever want to be a leader - serve. And if you want to be a good servant, you must care about the people you serve, and see them as important, valuable pieces of the puzzle that is your organization/family/community. If you can do that, you'll be surprised how easily people will follow. They may even ask: "how high?"

LEADERSHIP = INVESTMENT

In my research on leadership development I typically come across the same themes: qualities of effective leaders, elements of team building, etc. I've found, however, that a term germane to leadership is often missing:

Investment.

The concept is so fundamental to leadership development that it is often overlooked. When I mention it in my workshops, I often see that flicker of light in the eyes of my audience members as they reconnect to this simple truth: there is no leadership without investment in those who are led.

Often, "money" is the first thing that comes to the audience's mind when I mention that leaders must invest in those they lead. And they are correct. In order to get to know people, find out what makes them tick, learn their strengths and weaknesses in order to effectively task them, one must spend money. As an example, when I became Executive Director of a non-profit in Boston, one of the first things I did was take my entire staff out to see a movie and then to a local eatery for dinner and drinks, on my dime.

I found the investment to be worth every penny. Not only did the movie help to bond us (I took them to see "Amistad," which provided much heartfelt discussion afterwards), but it allowed us to talk to one another as men and women; people instead of just colleagues. And nothing bonds people more than food and beverage. We learned more about our common interests and differences in that one night than many had in years of working together. Finally, the next day, I bought each staff member a violet for their desks (you'd have to see the movie to understand the significance).

That relatively small investment allowed me to quickly get to know my staff, while they in turn got to see what makes me tick. That knowledge proved invaluable in forming trust between us, and gave me the insight to not only effectively task each staff member, but to know who needed training and development in which areas.

Although the importance of money cannot be understated when examining leadership and team development, I'd say that an even more important commodity must be invested by leaders: time. There is no substitution for it. Effective leaders inherently know that 20 minutes discussing the health of someone's close family member, even during busy work hours, can do more to build a productive team than cracking the proverbial whip. Your time may be spent saying a prayer over the phone with a friend who has called you out of the blue, or taking the time to listen to a community member who tells you why he needs change for the bus. It may be spent listening to a frustrated teacher who calls you for help with educating your child. In other words, while people often think that leadership development is only a work/career thing, I submit to you that you are part of many teams: workers on the job; family members; the community; your local school, etc. Time is the key ingredient to be invested in all of them.

For those of you who see yourselves or wish to see yourselves as effective leaders, I have but one question: how much do you invest in your teams?

LEADERSHIP DEVELOPMENT THROUGH OPPORTUNITY

There are very specific and well-documented methodologies used to develop leaders. Companies spend tremendous amounts of money annually to sponsor training sessions, workshops, retreats and the like for such purpose. Trainers are well versed in tried and true strategies, which they impart to their charges with the hopes that at least some will take the knowledge gained in their workshops and implement them in real ways and on a consistent basis.

Having said that, I've found that one of the most effective ways to develop leaders is to simply provide them with opportunities. The interesting thing is, you may be conscious of providing such opportunities, or you may not.

For instance, when I developed The Berlack Method, I wasn't thinking of developing specific leaders or providing anyone with leadership opportunities. I was thinking of my business as a one man show, with me doing all of the topic development and facilitation work. But one day, while discussing The Berlack Method with my sister, Verna Fludd Johnson, she mentioned to me that I should seriously consider starting a Facebook group page. After several hours of discussing the potential benefits of such a page, both to the company and to the people who would be members, I told her that I would indeed consider it.

After several days, I had not as yet begun work on the page. When my sister inquired about it, I truthfully told her that I was enthused about starting the page, but had been busy with work. That's all I needed to say, apparently. My sister, without encouragement from me, told me bluntly that the page will be created and not to worry about it. Within hours, she alerted me to check online and find my new page: The Berlack Method Group. I was astounded to find that the group already included several members, and they were already interacting and discussing topics related to my workshops. The co-creator and early administrator of the group was Maria Garrett, a close friend of my sister's whom I had never met personally. The two of them did all of the work, including gathering information, preparing and implementing the banner display, posting group rules for interaction, inviting the initial members, etc. I was astounded, and quite humbled, to see that I was no longer the only leader in The Berlack Method.

Very early in the group's history, a dear friend, Shauna Carter, became a group administrator. I had no idea what a God-send she would be. Initially, because the group bared my name, I felt wholly responsible for it, and made a point of continuously posting topics for discussion and generally interacting with members. As I became busier with development work for The Berlack Method, however, I had less time to devote to the group. From time to time I would pop back in to post or check out what was going on, and over time, I was again astounded. Not only had the group flourished, but it has now grown to over 1,300 members and counting. Shauna, without encouragement from me, became the leader of the group, posting many times daily, from deep, emotional topics for discussion, to frivolous, light-hearted pictures meant to lighten members' days, to music videos to jam to. Others followed suit, so that now the group has its "usual suspects" that can be counted on the keep the members hopping with news, entertainment, serious discussion, helpful tips, camaraderie, support for members who are struggling with different issues/life events, and even love.

As I continue to jump into the Berlack Method Group water and wade around from time to time, I am humbled to know that the group that bares my name is not about me. Through no conscious effort of mine, leaders like Verna, Maria and Shauna have taken their administrative places within the group, and are having a tremendous daily impact on the lives of over 1,300 people across the country. Members who have lost loved ones now post to the group for support. People struggling with issues of faith, family, politics or community now engage the group for ideas. Members peruse the group's posts for news, or sit in while other members host a Berlack Method Group throwback jam session, posting music videos from back in the day, and laughing at each other about old hair styles and dance moves.

As one of my last surprises, I happened to visit the group one day to find that we had a new banner. It sat bright and proud at the top of the group page, and I was astounded at how much I loved it, and how I had nothing to do with its creation or implementation. The group truly was its own entity. Though it bares my name, The Berlack Method Group is a reflection of its true parents: Verna Fludd Johnson, Maria Garrett and Shauna Carter. They are leaders who needed nothing more than an opportunity to shine. And shine they did, to the tune of helping over a thousand people get through the day with some joy, laughter, friendship, knowledge and love. Who knows how many family and friends of Berlack Method Group members are positively impacted day to day?

Come on by and see the work of true leaders: https://www.facebook.com/groups/180828168633066/

Developing leadership is a gift. But sometimes, developing leaders is simply a matter of providing opportunities for people to shine. Even if you aren't conscious of being a developer of leaders, take action. Do what you are purposed to do. Who knows what leaders will take their place by your side?

JAMES WELDON JOHNSON LIFTED MORE THAN HIS VOICE

I saw his name for the first time when I walked into a project complex in Harlem. A sign with huge letters at the front entrance read: "Welcome to the James Weldon Johnson Houses." I never heard of him. I was 27 years old. Being naturally curious, I looked him up on the internet, and found a lot of information on him in Wikipedia. What I read astonished me.

Born in 1871 in Florida, Johnson grew to become a true Renaissance Man. He taught himself Spanish and became U.S. Consul to Venezuela and Nicaragua. He became the first Black Executive Secretary of the N.A.A.C.P. He wrote a novel entitled "The Autobiography of An Ex-Coloured Man," and published a collective work called "Fifty Years And Other Poems." His most well-known work, however, was the poem that his brother J. Rosemond Johnson put to music. The piece was entitled "Lift Ev'ry Voice And Sing," known by many as "The Negro National Anthem."

This was all done by a Black man in the early years of the 20th Century.

The more I read about him, and the more I read his work, the more he influenced my thinking. Newly armed with awareness of all this man had accomplished, I could not allow any obstacles in my own life to hold me down. I found that the yearnings I had to explore my creativity and activism were validated by precedent. I no longer felt strange because of any "lack of focus" on a particular life path. Given this freedom, I went on to become active in my community, become an administrator in several major public agencies, host a nationally syndicated talk show, express my inner thoughts through poetry and am now writing a book on what I'd learned in life under the personal development banner of the company I founded.

I have a role model. Though he never met me, though he never thought about me personally, James Weldon Johnson has led me to great works. Even his death in 1938 could not stop his influence on my life. I have since made it a point to tell people about him whenever I can. I am sure that if he can lead me to unlock my mind, he can lead others to do the same if they are aware of him.

James Weldon Johnson is a leader by definition and by fact. He's had no authority over me. He held no title to which I've been bound. Yet his life is the example that developed the man I am.

Thank you sir. I pray to pass it forward.

CHAPTER 10

Community Impact

"The body is a community made up of its innumerable cells or inhabitants." – Thomas A. Edison

"I'm a reflection of the community." – Tupac Shakur

Author's Notes:

The term "community" is defined by www.dictionary.reference.com thus:

1. a social group of any size whose members reside in a specific locality, share government, and often have a common cultural and historical heritage.
2. a locality inhabited by such a group.
3. a social, religious, occupational, or other group sharing common characteristics or interests and perceived or perceiving itself as distinct in some respect from the larger society within which it exists (usually preceded by the): the business community; the community of scholars.

It is interesting to note that the term references both people and their location. Inherent in each definition is the idea that something, be it location, government, cultural heritage or interests, is shared by the people within it. To take it a step further, the elements of a community that are shared are often tied to self-identity, and for that reason are fundamental to values and to sense of worth. Definition 3 makes the important point that communities do not stand alone.

Most communities are, in fact, part of larger groups. As these societal units get larger, the idea of commonality gets more diffuse, and the ties that bind grow weaker. Therein lies the challenge of understanding the concept of community. Where does a community begin? Where does it end? At what point does my community become different from yours? Typically, the defining markers of community are man-made and un-natural. For instance, geographically speaking, what is the difference between northern Mexico and southern Texas? Yet, in spite of some cultural similarities, there are significant political, socio-economic and linguistic differences between the two. This fundamental challenge to the understanding of community often leads us to treat each other with everything from indifference to outright hatred. It is often the notion that one is considered part of the "other" group that leads one to experience the darker side of human nature. I submit to you, however, that our community shortsightedness is a matter of perspective. For instance, to the human ear, English may sound very different from Mandarin Chinese. But how similar would they sound compared to…say…Martian? If we were visited by extraterrestrials, would we as Americans then view Egyptians or Russians as so different? I think not.

My community growing up was The Bronx, New York. "Where I'm from" was one of the first things I learned as a child: starting with my address. It was one of my first sources of self-identification. The burned-out buildings and garbage on the streets were indicators of self-worth that I had to battle early on. Thankfully, I had a strong family network that buffered me from the negatives of the neighborhood, and opened me to the positives.

What was very interesting to me was that the neighborhoods I grew up in were often split between the Puerto Rican and African-American communities. I noticed very early in life that the two rarely converged, except in places like school. More importantly, citizens of these neighborhoods almost always focused on their differences, and rarely got along. It wasn't unheard of for fights to break out with my schoolmates along cultural lines. It wasn't until I learned of my familial ties to both cultures that I started to see the similarities. As an adult, my studies of history and culture revealed our common roots. In fact, my roots to Africa go through Puerto Rico, and not through the United States.

As a Christian, my understanding of community went to another level entirely. Several years ago, not long after I was baptized, I walked down the street in my neighborhood and realized that I saw people differently. Instead of seeing color, culture or gender, I saw people as souls living an earthly experience. Concepts such as nationality and race lost their significance. If I kept my thinking on the spiritual plane, then I saw everyone as part of my community. We all share *something* in common. More importantly, we don't all have to be aware of our commonality in order for it to exist. Think of it this way: If I gave you my telephone number and asked you to call me, would you have to build a line to my house, or build a tower to my cell? Of course not, the connection *already exists.* You simply don't have the number.

This chapter on community is part of the book because, I believe, positively impacting the community is the ultimate test of whether or not we are broadcasting our inner champions. If we do not impact others during our lifetimes, then why are we here? What's the point of learning anything, if we don't teach others? Why bother learning other languages, eating different foods, learning cultural dances, and debating different world views if none of it brings us closer as a human family?

However, in the effort to impact others, there is inherent danger. Before you engage in cultural discourse, you must know yourself. You must be rooted in self-awareness and in your own community. How can we connect with other cultures without understanding our own first? If I was not rooted in my identity as a Black, Puerto Rican American male, I would simply absorb the language and culture of anyone I interacted with during my travels in life. I would then find it difficult to connect with the people I grew up with. My sense of community impacts how I deal with personal relationships, how I work with others, and even how I parent my children.

My writing in the community chapter was often influenced by stories I came across in the media. Oddly enough, I found that many political stories were, in fact, tied to community ideals. You'll therefore find quite a few posts in this chapter dealing with politicians and their actions. I also want to point out that there are a number of posts outlining my activities in the community. I did that specifically to shed light on some of the wonderful events that take place in our communities daily, that don't always get the benefit of media coverage. I'll address that point again when we discuss next steps in The Epilogue.

"The Lion Speaks of the Enemy Within" came to me while listening to "War" by Bob Marley. The lyrics are taken directly from a Haile Selasie speech in 1964. Being the nerd that I am, I researched the speech while still listening to the song, and was floored by what I read. Every once in a while, someone speaks to me with such truth that I never forget it. King Selasie's speech rang with such truth.

The story that influenced "When Benevolence is Greater than Greed" struck me because the subject's actions flew in the face of the American ideal of "pulling oneself up by one's own bootstraps." Though this ideal certainly holds merit and has its place in our culture, I believe that an expanded and spiritually mature sense of community pushes us to think of more than just ourselves or our perceived parochial connections.

As a former educator, I was compelled to write "It's Time for Schools and Communities to Step Up." I am clear that without parental and community support, our children will continue to fail miserably both in academics and in life. Too often we as a community look for public schools to raise our children, and we forget the idea that parents are the first educators. We must unite with our schools, and make them more than just education centers. This is not just a community issue, but increasingly an issue of national importance and security.

So, who is part of your community? Where does your community end and others begin? Do you simply concern yourself with your personal interests and those of your family, or is the well-being of a family across the country of concern to you as well? Do you have a responsibility for anyone's well-being besides your own? If so, for whom do you bear such responsibility? What is the *source* of your responsibility? These questions are posed for your consideration as you read this chapter. May the boundaries of your community expand before your eyes and mind as you read.

WE MUST RESIST

David Starkey, a British national and an historian by trade, created a racial storm recently on BBC2. Appearing on the show "Newsnight," Starkey claimed that the recent riots in London and other social ills can be traced directly to the idea that White "chavs" (a British colloquialism for "aggressive, thuggish teenagers") have "now become Black," and have embraced Black culture. His exact words:

"A substantial section of the chavs has become Black. The Whites have become Black. A particular sort of violent, destructive, nihilistic, gangster culture has become the fashion."

See an article about Starkey and his comments here. http://www.dailymail.co.uk/news/article-2025554/David-Starkey-says-Enoch-Powell-right-infamous-rivers-blood-speech.html

Starkey didn't stop there. When confronted about his comments by other guests on the show and in the face of scathing rebuttals from the public, Starkey had this to say:

"I said until I was blue in the face on the programme that I was not talking about skin colour but gang culture. A large group of whites have started to behave like blacks. I think that is the most unracial remark anyone can make."

When I read about Starkey, several points came to mind. The first was that no matter how much legislation is passed, and no matter who is elected President of the U.S.A., people like David Starkey still have a world view based on racist beliefs and assumptions. His second quote demonstrates that logic and legislature can have minimal impact on perspective. I've said this before and I'll say it again - you can't legislate people's beliefs.

The second point that occurred to me was that it seems as if the election of President Obama has brought these ideas and world views out for public viewing and discussion. Before 2008, there were those of us who were of the mind that racism had become a thing of the past. To them, the election of President Obama proved it. They believed that because police no longer used dogs to attack throngs of people, or that because Black people no longer hung in Southern trees, that we had somehow turned a corner on race relations.

Have we made progress since the days of W.E.B. DuBois, Booker T. Washington, Ida B. Wells, Malcolm X and Dr. King? Certainly. Like a virus however, racism has mutated into the thing it has become. Resistant to old cures and strategies, racism didn't disappear so much as it found out where to thrive: in dark corners of private homes and at old family dinner tables. It learned that it could survive better by changing from loud and violent to quiet and deadly. Until now....

It also occurred to me that David Starkey serves as a reminder that racism is not an American issue alone. It is a human condition. This condition strikes us irrespective of nationality, culture or language. It thrives in private homes and dinner tables around the world. And it's getting loud again. If we're not careful, it will get violent...again.

That brings me to the final point that occurred to me. No matter how comfortable we may have become, no matter how tired we may be of "playing the race card," (I don't have the space or time to explain how ridiculous that phrase is to me), *we must resist* racism whenever and wherever it is found. By "we" I mean all of us. Irrespective of race, nationality, culture or language, we must stay true to our heritage as a human family, and protect one another from the virus that's plagued us since before recorded history.

Southern trees still sway in the wind. But *we* must determine what fruit they bear.

THE JACKIE ROBINSON OF AMERICAN POLITICS

On April 15, 1947, Jackie Robinson made his Major League debut, breaking the unwritten but all-too-visible color line. Branch Rickey, General Manager of the Brooklyn Dodgers and the visionary behind this move, had the foresight to recognize the tremendous untapped talent represented by African-American ballplayers. Ignoring social norm, Rickey placed winning above racial divides and hatred. More importantly, Rickey anticipated that Robinson would have to do much more than win on the diamond with his running, fielding and hitting.

Rickey knew that as the first to break the color line, Robinson would face day after day of vicious insults, players refusing to play with him on the field, hotels refusing him service, death threats, and more. On the field, Robinson would face pitchers throwing at his head, opponents crashing into him spikes-first, and with a torrent of racial slurs and epithets directed at him loudly and unashamedly. Robinson, in short, would have to be more than an exceptional ballplayer. He would have to be an exceptional man, standing tall in a hailstorm of hatred, ostensibly so that no other "colored" player would have to endure the same.

We all (should) know the rest of the story. Today, Mr. Robinson is in the baseball Hall of Fame, not only for his statistics (which alone would have placed him in the Hall), but for his role as an American hero and icon. In 1997, in an unprecedented move befitting his accomplishments, Major League Baseball retired Robinson's number 42 for all teams.

Fifty-one years after Robinson broke the MLB color barrier, Senator Barack Obama did the same in American politics when he became *President* Obama. Fifty-one years after Mr. Robinson endured a racially charged, hellish quagmire that many of us would fail to navigate, President Obama is enduring a constant, withering attack not just on his policies and politics, but on his place of birth, his nationality, his work ethic, his race, his religion, and more. In public and in open forum, including in the chambers of Congress, President Obama has been called a liar, lazy, a Muslim (I still don't see how that would be a crime), a terrorist sympathizer and more. The only thing left would be to openly call him the "N" word. Who knows what he's being called in private. His enemies have thrown political hard balls directly at his head, and have come at him spikes-up. And yet, in the tradition of Jackie Robinson, President Obama has stood tall. He has demonstrated an incomprehensible level of patience and self-control that many of us would fail to muster. Somewhere in his heart and mind, he must realize that he *has* to endure this, if only so that the next Presidents who are not White and male won't have to. Both Mr. Robinson and President Obama had strong and courageous wives to help them endure. But there is no Branch Rickey for President Obama. There is no Old Guard member of the establishment to turn it on its ear by introducing him to the world and standing by his side. He is the American President, leader of the free world, and he stands alone.

One jaw-dropping insult came when Colorado Congressman (R) Doug Lamborn equated being involved in negotiating policy with President Obama as being stuck to a "tar baby."

See article regarding this incident here. http://www.huffingtonpost.com/2011/08/01/doug-lamborn-colorado-con_n_915382.html?ref=fb&src=sp

While this story has been largely ignored by the national media, African-American outlets have rightly brought this to light, and Americans have responded. Congressman Lamborn's office phones have been flooded with angry messages and calls for his resignation. Some Americans disagree with the idea that Congressman Lamborn's statement constituted an attack, and don't understand the level of anger surging within the African-American community. For those that don't, I offer this statement:

PRESIDENT OBAMA IS THE JACKIE ROBINSON OF AMERICAN POLITICS.

While the community rises up in arms in anger and resentment, what does our President do? Research it. In short, he has simply ignored it. Look for any response on the part of the White House to this attack. Look at President Obama's responses as he's suffered indignities unheard of for an American President. Then think of Mr. Robinson and his ability to shine his positive spirit over all of the hatred and vitriol. Then look at our President again.

May we as Americans never see this level of disrespect for our President again. No matter what *she* looks like.

WHEN BENEVOLENCE IS GREATER THAN GREED

As a motivational speaker, I am always telling my audience to "broadcast your inner champion." By that, I mean for them to explore and identify who they are. I remind them that they must know their familial and cultural connections and how those connections make them who they are. Having done that, I then ask them to explore how to branch those connections and lessons learned out to others, thereby "broadcasting" their self-awareness, and demonstrating the responsibility that comes with understanding those connections.

In short, our lives, at their greatest, provide benevolence for people *other* than ourselves. It is the pinnacle of the concept of yin and yang, of reciprocity and living in spirit and purpose.

As much as I have trained to do this, and as much as my life experiences have prepared me to teach these concepts, every once in a while I am humbled by someone who *lives* them. I was so humbled when I read about Allan Guei in the July 29, 2011 edition of *The Week* magazine (*It Wasn't All Bad - page 2*). From the article: *Mr. Guei, a Compton High School graduate in Los Angeles, won a free-throw contest - earning a $40,000 college scholarship. Later, however, he received a basketball scholarship to California State University - Northridge.*

Mr. Guei was under no obligation to return the money earned from the free-throw contest. So what did he do? Instead of keeping it for himself (aren't we taught to maximize our profits at all costs?), Mr. Guei donated the contest money to the seven runners-up. Here's what he had to say:

"I've already been blessed so much and I know we're living with a bad economy. This money can really help my classmates."

Yes, as Americans we are taught to pull ourselves up by our own bootstraps, protect our individual and family interests, and let the other guy worry about the other guy. If "Other Guy" falls, then it was his fault anyway.

So why care? Well, thanks to Mr. Guei, we are reminded that one person falling is *everyone's* problem, either directly or indirectly. He also reminds us that when benevolence is greater than greed, America becomes better today than it was yesterday…and we come that much closer to the dream promised in our Declaration of Independence. So go ahead Mr. Guei, broadcast your inner champion.

THE LION SPEAKS OF THE ENEMY WITHIN

On October 4, 1963, H.I.M. Haile Selassie I of Ethiopia gave a speech at the United Nations that has reverberated in the actions of conscientious thinkers to this day. King Selassie made an impassioned plea to a world that perceived itself as disconnected from the injustices taking place in Africa at the time. He cautioned them to understand that the same instinct for survival and the same willingness to fight for justice and equality runs through all of us, irrespective of race, creed or color.

His message can only be done justice by his own words:

"…until the philosophy which holds one race superior and another inferior is finally and permanently discredited and abandoned: That until there are no longer first-class and second class citizens of any nation; That until the color of a man's skin is of no more significance than the color of his eyes; That until the basic human rights are equally guaranteed to all without regard to race; That until that day, the dream of lasting peace and world citizenship and the rule of international morality will remain but a fleeting illusion, to be pursued but never attained; And until the ignoble and unhappy regimes that hold our brothers in Angola, in Mozambique and in South Africa in subhuman bondage have been toppled and destroyed; Until bigotry and prejudice and malicious and inhuman self-interest have been replaced by understanding and tolerance and good-will; Until all Africans stand and speak as free beings, equal in the eyes of all men, as they are in the eyes of Heaven; Until that day, the African continent will not know peace. We Africans will fight, if necessary, and we know that we shall win, as we are confident in the victory of good over evil…"

On the surface, King Selassie, affectionately known as "The Lion," makes an eloquent comment on the human propensity to fight for what is right. Moreover, he not-so-vaguely hints that God sanctions "the good fight." This is not much different from a famous quote attributed to U.S. Navy Chaplain Howell Forgy on the U.S.S. New Orleans during the Japanese attack on Pearl Harbor:

"Praise the Lord and pass the ammunition."

Reading both quotes, it would be easy to believe that the "enemy" was the Japanese, or White racists, or other African leaders with oppressive regimes. But The Lion reaches deeper, and reveals to us that the real oppressor is The Enemy Within: malicious and inhuman self-interest. The true enemy is our inability to connect the fortunes of others to the fortunes of ourselves. One might argue that bigotry and prejudice should be included as The Enemy Within, but I submit that those malignancies are mere symptoms of self-interest.

Until the day we finally heed The Lion's words, the progress of the human race as evidenced by the election of an African-American as leader of the free world, will always be followed by the malicious backlash of those in power, spawned and fueled by self-interest. The progress of the human race as evidenced by the American outpouring of love and brotherhood in the aftermath of 9/11 will always be followed by outcries against the spread of Islam in a nation dedicated to the freedom of religion.

These things will always occur, until, in the words of King Selassie, the self-interest that drives these malicious deeds is "replaced by understanding and tolerance and good will...." I say today that such understanding cannot occur until we as a human race internalize the message that we are all together in this life-struggle.

The fight is not amongst nations. The fight is not against tyrants. The fight is not even, at its core, against racism and bigotry. The fight is with ourselves. The fight is against our very instinct to disconnect from that which we don't understand, or those who don't look, speak or think like us.

If we want to save ourselves from the war that King Selassie warns us about, then we must begin by connecting the fates, fortunes and families of others to our own. After all, are we not, at our core, one family?

And if King Selassie's words were too eloquent for some to understand, Bob Marley made the message perfectly clear: until the day we heed The Lion…there will be WAR.

THE PRICE OF A SOUL IN POLITICS

I was recently alerted to a political campaign attack ad that, upon viewing, transported me back about 100 years or more. I'd never seen a political ad so blatantly vicious, racist, sexist and hurtful. It would be difficult to describe my reaction. In short, I was speechless. And those that know me well know that that is indeed a rare occurrence.

See article and video here. http://talkingpointsmemo.com/dc/in-ca-36-democrat-calls-for-blanket-condemnation-of-stunning-new-web-ad-video

The video is so outlandish, it's hard to describe with words. A recently registered PAC by the name of *Turn Right, USA* produced a video mocking California 36th Congressional District candidate Janice Hahn's efforts to recruit former gang members to clean up the streets of Los Angeles by reforming other gang members. Janice Hahn is a Democrat. Using a strategy designed to motivate Republican voters, the video uses almost every available stereotype known in America. It depicts a model (supposedly Hahn), in a bikini, dancing on a pole, bending over and shaking her butt with dollar bills on it. Two Black men, sporting AK47's amongst other things, rap/sing out to the dancing "Hahn": "Give us your money B&*#%$ so we can shoot up the streets!"

The video then goes *completely* over the top, showing a close up of Hahn with shining red eyes, which harkens to a comment made recently by Tea Party Express Founder and Chairman Mark Williams:

"Each of us must vow to recognize that the letter "D" after a politician's name is a metaphorical Mark of the Beast, inasmuch as that party is now a wholly owned subsidiary of the domestic enemy, and that to repair and make again effective the Republican Party we must each do our part to take control of that party, not step away from it."

Check out "Teamwork Makes The Nightmare End" in the Achieving with Others chapter for more on this.

Then, to top it all off, the ad ends by morphing from the edited image of Hahn to one of an AK47 spraying bullets at some imaginary target. In light of the Gabrielle Giffords incident, and especially considering the environment some suspect was created by Sarah Palin's use of maps with gun targets on Democratic politicians prior to it, this video goes beyond ignorant to stunningly malicious.

For his part, the Republican candidate for the C-36 seat, Craig Huey, himself a Tea Party member, denounced the video, insisted his campaign had nothing to do with it, and demanded that *Turn Right USA* remove the video, which they promptly refused to do.

To get the full measure of what I'm describing, you really have to watch the video. Once I watched it, it took a while for me to even process what I saw. My first reaction was anger and disappointment, but I couldn't figure out why. Then it hit me....

It occurred to me that being upset with *Turn Right USA* was a waste of time. It also occurred to me that being upset with Huey, and/or figuring out to what extent he was involved would be equally frustrating and unfruitful. What did anger me, however, and what caused me the most pain, was the fact that the two Black men in the video actually agreed to be part of it! I mean...really??

I can only imagine money as the motivator for these two men to agree to being portrayed this way in the 21st Century. Many of us know what it's like when money is tight and we have to sacrifice to put food on the table, but who reading this would sell their soul, pride and dignity for money?

How much does it cost to buy a man's soul? How can these men, under *any* circumstance at this point, look their sons or daughters in the eye? How can they look any other family member in the eye, or any member of their community? How long will it take them to spend the money that put them in the middle of this time warp to the American Nightmare? And once it's spent, where will they be then??

As a father of two beautiful Black women-to-be, I know in my heart of hearts that I will never give up my soul that way. There isn't enough money in the world to cause me to do something that makes me unable to look them in the eye. I will always demonstrate, to the best of my ability, what a strong, proud, *American* man looks like. I *owe* them that. I owe them my soul, because their existence brought me closer to God in the first place, and to a true understanding of my connection to Him and to my fellow man. It's their existence, and the existence of those who've come before me, that define me as a man, and charge me to uphold my dignity and guard my soul.

I watched the video again, and couldn't help but remember the character of "Baines" in the movie *X*, describing us as lost in the wilderness. It pains me to no end that a movie character could describe Black men such as these so accurately. To the Brothers in the video…you are LOST. And the fact that you are lost *has been televised*. Come back to the American Revolution… throw that money back in *Turn Right's* face, look your sons and daughters in the eye again…and reclaim your souls.

THE STATE OF BLACK MEN IN AMERICA

It was my honor to be a guest on Real Talk with host Phoenix Starr on www.svmixradio.com. The topic of discussion was the state of Black men in America. Considering that it was a one hour show, we could not, of course, fully explore all that such a complicated subject entails. But we did tackle a lot of issues, with impassioned stories told, statistics presented and blueprints for future action to address said issues.

One of the first things we addressed was the idea that despite all of the challenges, there are some positive stories to tell about Black men. We are involved in our families, we have taken leadership of our communities, we have gotten involved in the political arena, we are educated and we are working. Heck, we're even President of the United States. However, the major challenge is that we're not doing these things at scale, and a significant percentage of us are struggling mightily: socially, politically and economically.

The statistics quoted on the show were alarming, and we began by addressing the penal system. Many people don't realize that the prison system alone is a 37 BILLION dollar industry. There are people making money off the fact that America has the highest incarceration rate in the world, with a prison population of over 2.3 million people. How does this affect Black men? Although Black people in this country as a whole represent 12% of the population, 35.4% of the prison population are Black males! Roughly 10% of all Black males are in prison. This number does not represent the rest of the penal system, i.e.: probation and parole. If this were happening to people who owned television stations and fortune 500 companies, it would be declared a national crisis, and we'd all be aware of the numbers, and we would *demand* that something be done about it as of yesterday.

We also compared those numbers to the education system. In 2000, 25% of Black men between the ages of 18-24 were in college. Compared to the percentage of men in prison, one might think "not bad," except when that number is compared to the rest of society: 35% of Black women in the same age group were in college, and 36% of the overall population in the same age group were in college. As of 2010, only 35% of Black men actually graduated from college. These numbers are appalling.

We also discussed the continuing impact of slavery on the Black male. Today, many Americans simply don't want to hear this, and even have a term for it: "pulling the race card." Personally, I think that's an ignorant statement at best, and in itself is racist at worst. As a former history teacher, I am all too aware of the impact of studying our history in order to understand our present and our future direction. We've all heard the term: "those who don't know their history are doomed to repeat it." So why do so many Americans hate for us to continue to discuss the impact of slavery? I think the answer is obvious, but I don't care to use this forum to try to convince anyone.

What I can say is that as a historian I've studied the impact of slavery on our community. I know that a slave woman who was raped by her "master" had some strong feelings towards her husband, who was powerless to stop her torture and humiliation. As a man, I can only imagine how watching the abuse of my wife would impact my male ego, particularly in such a personal and sexual way, literally right in my face. So, what do *you* think these parents passed on to their children about gender roles and the state of the Black man? What impact do *you* believe that had on the respect Black women had for Black men? Do you really need a doctoral degree and thousands of pages of research to know the answer?

We also discussed why there is an achievement gap between Black men and women. There's lots of research on this, and you're free to look it up for yourself. What I'll say is this: as a student at Andover I had a moment of education I've never forgotten, and it occurred outside the classroom. My roommate, who was a White male from Valley, Nebraska, was walking along the campus with me one day. A Black girl walked past us, and my roommate asked me if she was "considered pretty." At first I was livid. How could he *not* see how beautiful she was? (I had a HUGE crush on her, and yes, I still remember her name. Lord...high school days). But when I looked at his face, I realized that he was sincere in his asking. So I simply said: "Only you know if she's attractive. What do you think?" He responded that he was indeed attracted to her.

Because I answered him so calmly, he relaxed and told me something I never forgot. He said: "I've always been attracted to Black women, but I'm terrified of Black men." All of a sudden, for me, a lot of puzzle pieces fell into place. Of course, this is only anecdotal. But if you're unfamiliar with Andover, Google it. Graduates from this school have gone on to become U.S. Presidents, legislators, doctors, attorneys, business leaders, and a wide array of people in political and economic power. Do my former roommate's sentiments reflect those of Andover? I think not. But if even a small percentage of these powerful leaders felt as he did, then given their power and clout, what kind of impact has that had on Black men as a whole?

To continue, each of the guests on Real Talk gave anecdotal evidence about why they've been successful as Black men in their various fields and as family men. We discussed how to overcome such obstacles as individuals and as a community. As for me: 1) "there but for the grace of God go I." 2) My family was responsible for teaching me about who I am, where I come from, challenges my family has overcome, and what it means to be "a Berlack." No school can teach us these fundamental lessons.

We concluded with the idea that government and politics aside (America is the only industrialized nation whose majority believes that government has no role in equaling the societal playing field), it is incumbent upon *us* to take control of our own destiny. *We* must teach our children who they are. *We* must take control of our own economy and politics. And we, as men, must step up to the plate and become the leaders of our families and communities that we are built to be.

I founded The Berlack Method in order to be part of the solution. We must, however, collaborate and work together as individuals and as organizations to engender effective change. That's why I collaborated with Caprice Smith and SharperMinds Consultants to create the "Third Thursdays" series of community open forums, and that's why I've also collaborated with Harding Consulting to facilitate "GQ Camp for Boys" for young men aged 10 - 16. As I did last year, this summer I will teach young males about how to become *men*. I'll teach them fundamentals like how to tie a tie, the history of gender roles, including how they've evolved and what has never changed, and even how to use the game of chess as a life skills teaching tool.

I declare today that the state of Black men in America is one of constant progress and tremendous challenge, and that Black men face both inner and outer obstacles that are mountainous in stature. As a Black man in an

America with a Black President, I stand ready, willing and able to move the state of Black men from challenged to empowered. What are *you* willing to do?

SOME OF US JUST DON'T GET IT

Since I've been an adult, I've been conscious of the idea that a government can't legislate the hearts of its people. Never has that been clearer than with the recent actions of the Alabama Senate.

One hundred and fifty years after the start of The Civil War, and fifty years after the Freedom Riders took center stage in the Civil Rights movement, the Alabama Senate approved a bill that would eliminate language from its constitution that calls for poll taxes and separate schools for Black and White students. When I read this in the May 13, 2011 issue of *The Week* magazine (page 6), I was stunned. That's May 13, TWO THOUSAND AND ELEVEN.

It then hit me: when President Obama was elected as our nation's first African-American President, (the irony being that the history of American Black self-identification aside, he really *is* African-American), Alabama still had this language in its constitution. In fact, when a similar bill to eliminate such language passed in 2004, it was defeated in a statewide referendum.

So, with a Civil War won (well, I guess that depends on who one asks), civil rights legislation on the books, and a Black man as President of the United States, there are *still* states in this country dragging themselves kicking and screaming out of the 20th century. So what makes us so reluctant to join the present? Ultimately, we're so blinded by our lust for wealth and power that we stomp on those we perceive as threats to the same.

What's wrong with us? Some of us just don't get it. We are *all* connected. We are all responsible for one another. And until we all get it, we will continue to flounder in the nightmarish sidebar of the American dream. We will continue to stare at each other across the chasm of our overly-emotional and simplistic self-perceptions of what America is, and what America isn't. We will continue to have perceptions that are guided by emotion and centuries-old, hatred-tinged teachings, ignorant of the light and truth inside each of us.

The sad part is, while we Americans stare across that chasm at each other, other countries are lapping us in the do-or-die competition that is the world market. We're being out-American-ed. Countries we once scoffed at in the global economy ring are playing Cassius Clay to our Sonny Liston. Unless we "get it" soon, we'll find ourselves face-down on the canvas, and our American dream will turn into the nightmare of the "knocked out."

Come on America. We all want the American dream. But…"for what does it profit a man to gain the whole world and forfeit his soul?" (Mark 8:36)

THE GRAY LINE

Angelina Lange, a 17 year-old senior at St. Anthony's High School in Bay Shore, New York, was denied permission to take her ex-girlfriend to the prom. Her options: go by herself, find a male date, or stay home.

See newspaper article here. http://www.nydailynews.com/new-york/st-anthony-high-school-long-island-bars-lesbian-student-bringing-female-date-prom-article-1.146843

Brother Gary Cregan, Principal of the Roman Catholic school, had this to say:

"Our Catholic faith specifies that marriage involve a man and a woman, and our policies on dating must reflect that."

That's a very black line in white hot sand. Not much wiggle room. The good news is that the school (and the church) is very clear about this policy. We know where they stand on this. So…what's to argue about?

Legal issues aside (St. Anthony's is a private school and therefore has the right to determine policy regarding its events), this particular incident raises some interesting points about our connections to each other, our responsibility for one another, and how some of us use the Bible and religion to pass judgment on one another.

For instance, as a history student I researched the Ku Klux Klan. Imagine my surprise when I unearthed a KKK application from the 1920's, and discovered that in order to become a member, one had to declare himself a Christian. Thus the burning crosses. So, one has to be a Christian to hang people from trees? Is it Christian-like to roll hot irons over someone's body in a public square, literally peeling off someone's skin because he dared to vote while being a black man? (True incident - it occurred in front of the man's family, no less. See "Lynchings and Other Southern Horrors" by Ida B. Wells to learn more).

Here's my point: we can all clearly see that these things are not Christian-like. But the scary thing is, the men under those white sheets truly believed that they were right, and would quote chapter and verse to justify their beliefs and actions. This is not different than what we see (and are all impacted by) today with fundamentalist Islam. If anyone actually researches Islam, it is a religion of peace, with a belief in one Almighty God. (Sound familiar)? But to Al Qaida and the Taliban, the Qur'an is clear and simple justification for their belief that all infidels must die.

We can look to our own Bible (anyone here read Joshua?) to see examples of extreme action taken in the name of God. Joshua, armed with instructions from God given to Moses, killed every living being (man, woman and child) in the towns and villages of Canaan. Not only that, Joshua impaled several of the kings on sharpened poles and left their bodies up the entire day until sunset. He killed 31 kings in all. Now, if an American army went into a Middle Eastern village and killed every man, woman and child there, then impaled the local Al Qaida leader and left his body for all to see until sunset, what would we think about that? What would *they* think?

Getting back to the Catholic Church for a moment, are we to forgive the church for all of the incidents we've read about (and some experienced first-hand) concerning the rape and molestation of boys? Do we forgive the cover-ups by high-ranking church officials? How many of us heard those responsible for the cover-ups declare that they took action "for the good of the church," even at the expense of the boys? Should we always hold that against them? Do we call them on the carpet for that when they mention policy such as the one at St. Anthony's?

Because we are connected to one another, bound tightly by our roles as part of the body, we do have the responsibility to lead others to righteousness. It is part of our mission to be the examples of good for others to follow. But if I use one chapter and verse to call out the imperfections of one part of the body, can they not use another chapter and verse to call me out on the carpet about my own transgressions? Who here is so perfect that s/he can judge fairly? I only know one answer. God.

As for the rest of us, that very black line in white hot sand becomes awfully gray when seen through the lens of our humanity. Be careful. That lens will soon focus on you, and when it does, will you be able to look God in the eye and demand entry into heaven?

WHO'S BUYING THE COW?

One week from today, on Thursday May 19, 2011, Caprice Smith, President of SharperMinds Consultants and I will present the last in the "Third Thursdays" series of community open forums. The title for this one: "Who's Buying The Cow? Mr. & Mrs. vs. Baby Daddy & Baby Mama." It will be held, as has the others, at Pimlico Elementary/Middle School #223 in Baltimore, from 5:30 p.m. - 7:00 p.m.

We're greatly looking forward to this one! The buzz about the topic amongst my friends/family and on my social media networks has been high, to say the least. Needless to say, this is a great topic because it's not only timely, but the institution of marriage (or lack thereof) and the nuances of long-term relationships are issues that impact all of us. Just as important, these are issues that many of us feel very strongly about, one way or the other. Is it necessary to have a strong and healthy marriage in the home in order to have a strong and healthy family? Why are divorce rates so high in America today? What does the high divorce rate say about the typical American attitude towards marriage? What issues (if any) are presented by children in a household having multiple fathers? Why is father absenteeism so prevalent in certain communities and not in others? Will our children live with the same divorce rate as we are? What's the future of their long-term relationships?

We'll deal with these questions and many more during the forum. We're not only excited because of the great topic, but we're looking forward to seeing some of our audience regulars over the past few months. Our audiences have been fantastic! They've been vocal, communicative and *real* about all of the topics we've covered and then some.... As facilitator, I have yet to get through the questions I've prepared beforehand, because I'm usually following up with new questions generated by the audience. They've debated with respect and dignity, they've reluctantly agreed, and they've flat-out disagreed with each other. And we've all learned because of it. And that was the point.

The topics we've covered during this series:

- Parent Up! Who's Parenting Who?
- Does "No" Ever Mean "Yes?" Domestic Violence Exposed
- Enough Already! Stop Using The "N" Word!
- Who's Buying The Cow? Mr. & Mrs. vs. Baby Daddy & Baby Mama

When Caprice and I planned these forums last year, we had no idea, of course, how they would turn out. We envisioned audiences passionately debating issues with their community neighbors about important and hard-hitting issues, and that's exactly what happened. The Park Heights community has been phenomenal, and has supported us throughout. We look forward to working with them again in the near future, making "Third Thursdays" bigger and better next school year.

I wanted to take a moment to thank some great people for their efforts in making this happen. Kudos to:

Co-Presenters:

- The Berlack Method, LLC
- SharperMinds Consultants

Co-Hosts:

- Pimlico Elementary/Middle School #223
- Park Heights Renaissance, Inc.

Coordinators/Logistics:

- Elneeta Jones - Principal, Pimlico
- Jackie Peterson (Pimlico/Park Heights Renaissance, Inc.)
- Wanda Williams (Pimlico)
- Support Staff at Pimlico

We could not have made these fantastic forums happen without your loving help and support. THANK YOU!

This particular team came together to makes things happen and make a difference in lives we touch directly and indirectly. We stand with the conviction that we will continue to work tirelessly so that our results will get bigger and better as time goes on.

Where do you fit in this effort? Please start by supporting "Who's Buying The Cow…?" Let your voice be heard in your community! Then, what will you do from there?

THE WEDDING OR THE MARRIAGE?

When Caprice Smith and I planned the forum, "Who's Buying The Cow? Baby Daddy & Baby Mama vs. Mr. & Mrs.," we knew it was going to be explosive. With divorce rates over 33% for some segments of the American population, who's buying the cow indeed?

Here's a sample from www.divorcerate.org:

Age at marriage for those who divorce in America

Age	Women	Men
Under 20 years old	27.6%	11.7%
20 to 24 years old	36.6%	38.8%
25 to 29 years old	16.4%	22.3%
30 to 34 years old	8.5%	11.6%
35 to 39 years old	5.1%	6.5%

See more information about divorce rates here. http://www.divorcepad.com/rate/

What's interesting to note is that the divorce rates are in some ways reflective of a changing culture and climate concerning marriage in America. During my childhood in The Bronx, I only knew one classmate that grew up with both parents in the home. Needless to say, there are myriad issues at work here. The question, however, is this: what impact does all of this have on our attitudes towards marriage/long-term relationships? Further, what impact do our attitudes have on our children?

When I posted the question: "What's more important, the wedding or the marriage?" on my Facebook and Twitter pages, the responses flowed in like water. Almost all gave the quick response: "marriage." However, when I pushed back by asking why so much time, energy and money is spent on wedding ceremonies if the marriage is more important, the answers got a little HOT. Some people talked about The Cinderella Syndrome, The Big Letdown (great ceremony, fantastic honeymoon…back to real life…and NOW WHAT?!), previous bad relationships/marriages, their relationship with God, their need to love "self" first, and some mentioned that marriage was not a life goal at all.

Clearly, there is no easy answer to the question of whether the wedding or the marriage is more important. We all know what *sounds* good to say, but I don't think we'd see the divorce rates we're seeing now if the answer were that simple.

Stay tuned for the forum! This should be a good one.

So...what's *your* answer?

MENDENHALL CAUSES AMERICAN SELF-EXAMINATION

NFL star and Pittsburgh Steelers running back Rashard Mendenhall caused quite a stir when he tweeted comments contrary to popular opinion about Osama bin Laden's death and our reaction to it. Mendenhall, who is 23, commented first about a potential 9/11 conspiracy, tweeting: "We'll never know what really happened. I just have a hard time believing a plane could take a skyscraper down demolition style."

See article about his comments and media/popular reaction to them here. http://www.nydailynews.com/sports/football/rashard-mendenhall-embroiled-controversy-twitter-comments-osama-bin-laden-death-article-1.140320

The main focus of his comments, however, concerned American reaction to the news of bin Laden's death. Many people took to the streets across the country in an impromptu patriotic pep rally and party. We all saw the videos and pictures of people waving American flags, chanting "U.S.A.! U.S.A.!" and smiling brightly for group pictures. The atmosphere was electric, to say the least. It provided a moment that we're all likely to remember for the rest of our lives. It was a historic moment, to be sure.

What did Mendenhall have to say about all this?

"What kind of person celebrates death? It's amazing how people can HATE a man they have never even heard speak. We've only heard one

side... I believe in God. I believe we're ALL his children. And I believe HE is the ONE and ONLY judge. Those who judge others will also be judged themselves. For those of you who said you want to see Bin Laden burn in hell and piss on his ashes, I ask how would God feel about your heart?"

Wow. Talk about calling us all out. And to make his point even more powerful, there is plenty of scripture to back his points:

Mathew 7:1-5: (ESV)

Judge not, that you be not judged. For with the judgment you pronounce you will be judged, and with the measure you use it will be measured to you. Why do you see the speck that is in your brother's eye, but do not notice the log that is in your own eye? Or how can you say to your brother, 'Let me take the speck out of your eye,' when there is the log in your own eye? You hypocrite, first take the log out of your own eye, and then you will see clearly to take the speck out of your brother's eye.

Matthew 15:11 and 15-20 (NLT)

"You are not defiled by what you eat; you are defiled by what you say and do." Then Peter asked Jesus, "Explain what you meant when you said people aren't defiled by what they eat." "Don't you understand?" Jesus asked him. "Anything you eat passes through the stomach and then goes out of the body. But evil words come from an evil heart and defile the person who says them. For from the heart come evil thoughts, murder, adultery, all other sexual immorality, theft, lying, and slander. These are what defile you. Eating with unwashed hands could never defile you and make you unacceptable to God!"

There are plenty more scriptures about this, but the point is, Mendenhall has, at the very least, some powerful ground to stand on.

What Mendenhall expressed was his opinion, and certainly anyone may agree or disagree. The fact that some Americans disagreed with what he had to say isn't surprising or alarming. What was alarming was the media's response, and the response of some readers to what he had to say. The paper in which the above referenced article appears characterized Menhenhall as ranting, and even went so far as to suggest that he is ignorant. Readers called him everything from "idiot" to "ignorant" to racial slurs, and even called for Mendenhall to be cut from the team. Steelers owner Art Rooney, II had this to say:

"I have not spoken with Rashard so it is hard to explain or even comprehend what he meant with his recent Twitter comments, Rooney said. The entire Steelers' organization is very proud of the job our military personnel have done and we can only hope this leads to our troops coming home soon."

What I find interesting about Rooney's response is his need to include how proud the organization is of the troops, which provides a clue to this intense reaction. In times of war or economic hardship, history has shown that extreme political and social behavior becomes evident. We have both. For examples of what can happen, we need only look at Nazi Germany or Fascist Italy to understand. There's nothing wrong with being patriotic. Far from it. But there is something terribly wrong when a dissenting opinion is looked at as a measure of one's love of country.

Mendenhall reminds us to be careful, and to examine ourselves before we take to the streets, or drown each other out in our own shouting. We are *all* connected. We *all* matter, and a life is still a life. You're still an American if you don't chant "U.S.A.!" because someone lost his life.... Right?

LIFE IMITATES ART – PRESIDENTS OBAMA AND SHEPHERD

A movie that I've seen and enjoyed several times on cable is "The American President," starring Michael Douglas and Annette Bening. In what seems to be pure Hollywood storytelling, President Andrew Shepherd (Douglas), is a widower and single dad whose wife died of cancer three years earlier. He is roundly criticized by his Republican rival during an election year when it's discovered that President Shepherd is..."gasp!"...dating. The point of the attack is that Ms. Wade (The President's love interest played by Bening) has a controversial past in which she attended rallies many years before during which the flag was burned in protest. Not only is this brought out, but the President's morals and parenting abilities are publicly attacked because of it.

President Shepherd refuses to acknowledge the attacks or answer them, despite repeated and desperate attempts by his staff to do so, given his plummeting approval rating. Without giving away too much of the plot, the climax comes when the President finally has enough and gives a scathing retort in a press conference just before the State of the Union address. The theme of his response: being President is an incredibly serious job, with serious issues confronting him and his staff daily. The President points out that his rival does not have the moral compass to criticize someone whose service to her country includes decades of fighting for the very rights the rival was looking to shut down. More importantly, the issues that he as President must face make a focus on his private love life and her decades-old past seem utterly ridiculous and petty. In his speeches, the rival trumpets: "I am Bob Rumson and I'm running for President," to which the President finally replies: "We have serious issues and it takes serious men and women to handle them. These are serious times and your fifteen minutes are up. I'm Andrew Shepherd and I *am* the President!"

Amazingly, this is not far from what's happened with "The Birther" attacks on President Obama. I have never heard of an attack on the President as mundane and as far outside the real issues of the day as this one. With thousands of American soldiers losing their lives overseas, gas prices over $4 a gallon (at the time), high unemployment, another fight over states' rights 150 years after the start of the Civil War (this should be its own post), a battle over nationalized health care and who should or should not shoulder the tax burden and to what degree, I applaud the President this morning for finally addressing how idiotic it sounds to waste time discussing the President's place of birth.

President Obama is our President. Mine and yours. *Get over it already.*

I have no qualms with either Republicans or Democrats. The fact is, I see merit in each platform. However, the thing that voters really care about is that our elected officials act like grown-ups, get over their ideological differences and allow our connection as Americans to trump all other issues so that we may prosper as a nation. We are all connected! (Are you sensing a theme here)? The sooner we realize that, and the sooner we see the betterment of all elements of our society as the betterment of America, the sooner we can fulfill the promise of our great nation.

You may disagree with the President's politics and policies. You may believe in states' rights, big business and the limitation of the federal government, but that's the *President* you're talking to. Show him the respect he deserves, and debate him on real issues. As for all the other nonsense, your fifteen minutes are up.

THE WEEK OF THE "N" WORD

Last week was a great one for me intellectually, spiritually and business-wise. I had two distinct opportunities to publicly discuss an issue that continues to have a tremendous impact on America as a whole.

I had the honor of being a panelist on "The Simply Bonita Show" on www.svmixradio.com. The topic: "The 'N' Word." The theme centered on whether or not the African-American community should still use the word in conversation. The debate got heated (as one might expect), but everyone was respectful and articulated their opinions well. I'm typically the facilitator in such events, so I really enjoyed the opportunity to speak my mind on the issue without having to be concerned about "equal time." (It was Bonita's turn to worry about that)!

My thoughts? The word should be unequivocally tortured and executed, much like what has happened to many Americans under this particular word's banner. As a former U.S. History teacher, I am all too familiar with the atrocities committed with this word at the center. While still teaching, I was asked to write a poem (I love to write poetry and I've had the honor of blessing some open mics here in Baltimore) to commemorate Black

History Month. It was the first time I'd ever been asked to write something for a specific event, and I didn't know what to say. So for a week, I stood outside my classroom door and listened to my students as they walked the halls. I was appalled at how many times I heard the "N" word thrown about the building. I thought about Malcolm X and his assertion that we no longer needed to be physically chained because many of us had adopted "the slave mind."

The result was a poem called "Whose Nigga?" which explores in grim (and historic) detail the pain, torture, death and destruction dealt to Americans labeled by other Americans with that word. I was thinking about this poem when I spoke on Bonita's show. Sure enough, the argument was made that "a" is different than "er," and I responded to that with lines from another poem of mine called "A & ER."

The difference between A and ER
Is the difference between ignorance
And ignorance with malice

But which is more dangerous?
Malicious intent from the outside?
Or contaminated content from the inside?

The debate continued to ebb and flow, and many more profound points were made than I have room here to explore. But we all, panelists and guests alike, learned. It was a great evening.

The following night, Caprice Smith of SharperMinds Consultants and I presented the third in our "Third Thursdays" community open forum series, entitled: "Enough Already! Stop Using The 'N' Word!" This was another great opportunity for dialogue and cross-pollination of knowledge and ideas. As facilitator, my comments were limited, but the panelists and community guests were fantastic! Some of the same issues were brought to the forefront, but this event brought some twists to the debate: including the perception of Blacks from the Caribbean and other parts of the world concerning African Americans and their struggle with racism here. Everyone was active and lively, and the conversation continued long after the forum came to a close.

The most powerful moment for me came at the end when I did something off the cuff and a little different from the norm. I recalled for everyone another open mic piece I co-presented with Kurtis Watkins called "Words Give Birth." (Geez, recurring theme, anyone? I seem to have written a lot about this). During the presentation about the power of words, we placed a stand with the pictures of famous African American leaders such as Harriet Tubman, Martin Luther King, Jr., Ida B. Wells, Malcolm X, etc. on the stage. While I recited the poem, Kurtis, who had presented a similar piece the week before, spray painted in bright red the word "Niggas" over the pictures. We left the stand there the rest of the night, and nobody dared to move it. POWERFUL.

Having set the scene, I asked the panelists to close the forum by each channeling a leader, and describing to the audience how they felt about having that word painted over their pictures in front of an audience of their people, and whether or not it mattered that the word was spelled with an "A" instead of an "ER." The responses were real, emotional and extremely thought-provoking. What a way to end a forum. It was a great week.

As always, many kudos and thanks to: Bonita Linkins and the svmixradio. com crew, my co-presenter Caprice Smith, Forum Co-Hosts Pimlico Elementary/Middle School # 223 and Park Heights Renaissance, Elneeta Jones - Principal, Jackie Peterson and Wanda Williams of Pimlico, panelists Dalyn Allen, Dr. Renee Carr, Will Hanna and Mia Miata, and to all of the countless others who make these kind of events possible.

This was the week of the "N" word...may it rest forever...in peace or otherwise. What are your thoughts on this?

Steve Berlack

RADIO INTERVIEW ON WWW. NEWLIBERIAFM.COM

On Saturday, January 22, 2011, I had a great on-air interview with Host Wendy Hancils of www.newliberiafm.com.

We discussed issues impacting the large and active African community in the D.C./Maryland/Virginia area, Pan-Africanism, and the spiritual connection that binds all of us irrespective of race, creed or color. In particular, I spoke about the fact that my surname is a product of my Prussian Jewish ancestor, while my roots to Africa go through Puerto Rico instead of through the U.S. Talk about a mixed bag, but if that's not the American story, what is?

I also spoke about my Fulbright trip to Peru, during which I studied Afro-Peruvian and Andean history and culture. I remember well the meetings we scholars had with the elders of the Afro-Peruvian community, during which they told us of their struggles to remain rooted in their African ancestry while also engaging actively in Peruvian society.

Given the extensive reach of our connections to one another as I've described above, I believe it's important for us as Americans to pay close attention to the events in Tunisia and Egypt. The outcome of their protests and the Tunisian popular overthrow of the government will have far-reaching implications for us here in the States. It is in all of our interests to look past color, race and nationality in order to build liberty and democracy as one people.

Finally, we discussed The Berlack Method's inspirational workshops and community open forums, which touch on similar themes, such as our personal connections to and responsibility for one another.

By the way, I was *jamming* on an exotic mix of African, Caribbean, Old School R&B and House music played on Newliberiafm.com before my interview. I loved it and will be back for more.

Shout out to Wendy Hancils and the team at Newliberiafm.com for a job well done.

TAKE ACTION!

In Numbers 27: 12 - 13, God instructed Moses to climb a mountain east of the River Jordan, and gaze upon the Promised Land. God told Moses that he would die upon doing so. Knowing this, Moses did exactly as instructed. Dr. Martin Luther King, Jr., on the night before his death, said he had gone to the mountaintop, and his eyes had seen the "promised land." Knowing the dangers around him, and perhaps knowing his time to come home had arrived, Dr. King bravely continued to take action.

Unfortunately, many of the social issues Dr. King faced are still relevant today. According to Drs. William H. Cosby and Alvin Poissant in their book "Come On People":

* Homicide is the number one cause of death for black men between fifteen and twenty-nine years of age and has been for decades.

* Ninety-four percent of all black people who are murdered are murdered by other black people.

* In some cities, black males have high school drop-out rates of more than 50 percent.

There are even more statistics about the social ills impacting African-Americans (males in particular), and the poor (irrespective of race or gender) that are just as horrifying. This is why I decided to take action, and founded "The Berlack Method, LLC." I came to understand that I could talk about these issues, and go about my business day-to-day, or I could use my God-given gift of public speaking to *do* something about it. I stand ready to *take action* by facilitating community forums and other events, speaking to the masses in keynote addresses that tackle important issues of the day, using my writing talents in poetry and prose, and by training parents, youth and corporate staff to overcome the issues that have plagued us for decades and more.

I am prepared to engage community stakeholders in the kind of "uncomfortable conversations" that force us all to stand up, take notice, and take action. Our love for each other and for our communities is not enough - we must be honest in open conversation with one another and we must take conscientious action if we are to make real the sacrifices of Dr. King and Moses. They both went to the mountaintop knowing their deaths were near. Can we do any less for our children and our communities??

R.U.L.E.S. FOR BLACK MEN SYMPOSIUM

On Saturday, November 13, 2010, I had the distinct pleasure to be a panelist and presenter at the R.U.L.E.S for Black Men Symposium held on the campus of Morgan State University.

The Brothers of the Pi Chapter of Omega Psi Phi Fraternity, Inc. and the members of S.M.O.O.T.H. (Strong Men Overcoming Obstacles Through Hard-Work) produced this inspiring and educational event. Omega Psi Phi is, of course, an esteemed and historic organization for men, founded at Howard University in 1911. S.M.O.O.T.H., on the other hand, is a contemporary male student organization founded in the fall of 2009 to give members a place to grow academically, ethically and socially during their tenure at Morgan State University.

The symposium was open to the general public, and Morgan students attended as well. Job Corps brought teens and pre-teens in from Delaware and Maryland to gain fatherly and brotherly advice from the esteemed panel and workshop presenters.

I sat on the opening panel which discussed everything from the societal impact of fatherless homes to business advice to gender relationships in the Black community. Not surprisingly, the young audience peppered the panel with insightful questions on all topics. I was proud to be part of an inter-generational discussion that prayerfully laid a foundation of activism and communal concern in a group of future leaders.

I also presented a workshop entitled "Man Up!" which explored the history of the role of the Black male in our own community and in the greater American melting pot. I also instituted elements of The Berlack Method's personal development workshops to explore the role of discipline and accountability in the Black male's path to success in the future.

As always, I'm proud to serve the community in this way. There are strong, brave and ambitious young men out there who need the guidance and support of their elders. Thanks to Omega Psi Phi, S.M.O.O.T.H. and Morgan State University for providing a wonderful opportunity for all.

REAL TALK PANEL SERIES

On October 13, 2010, I had the honor to be a panelist for Morgan State University's Real Talk Panel Series. This edition of the series focused on business and entrepreneurial advice.

I shared the dais with thoughtful and engaging panelists that pulled on their years of experience to provide thought-provoking anecdotes and words of wisdom to eager students from The Earl G. Graves School of Business & Management. Our topics included general business tips, the role of networking, Morgan State's unique and expansive network, the joys (and perils) of entrepreneurship and more. As a former non-profit Executive Director, teacher, school administrator, media talent and current business owner, I found that I had much to say. I especially enjoyed connecting social and historical themes to the topic of business ownership. Student questions were incisive, to say the least, and challenged us on the panel to dig deep for answers.

Kudos to Morgan State University, the Office of Student Activities, The Student Government Association and The Earl G. Graves School of Business & Management for a wonderful and engaging discussion. I thoroughly enjoyed it and look forward to participating in similar events.

IT'S TIME FOR SCHOOLS AND COMMUNITIES TO STEP UP

Education Week posted a great article about the history of state interventions with struggling schools.

Steve Berlack

Original article is here. http://blogs.edweek.org/edweek/state_edwatch/2010/09/better_strategies_for_state_interventions.html

One statement in particular stood out:

"States have a better record of performing 'triage' during emergencies than in building the foundation for educational improvements, writes the author of the report, William J. Slotnick. And they're not particularly good at building the capacity of local communities to sustain the academic changes they make."

As a former educator in a major urban public school system, I couldn't agree more. However, I believe this statement only scratches the surface of the issue at hand.

My experience has been that state governments and school systems are ineffective at building the foundation for educational improvements because they are unwilling to engage their communities in tough love. Millions of dollars are poured into school systems: building infrastructure, training teachers, writing and re-writing curricula, re-training teachers and administrators on the hot new research-based strategies that weren't available the month before, and so on, and so on. Meanwhile, too many of our students are walking through multiple gang territories to get to school, struggle with parents who tell them in no uncertain terms that it's okay to disrespect their teachers if the teachers "disrespect" them (the *nerve* of some teachers to actually enforce school rules), and who bear witness to drug abuse, violence, fractured families, and more. Why would a student care about studying or removing his/her hat in a school building if s/he's *hungry*? When a student spends the night texting about a fellow student who was shot in the head, and e-mails the pic s/he took of him showing the bullet hole and blood everywhere, and then spends the next morning eating a bag of potato chips and calling that breakfast, s/he couldn't care less how well-trained the teachers are.

Until states are willing to spend millions of dollars fixing the problems that exist in the communities outside our schools, then we will continue to witness failing school systems. And until schools are willing to face their communities and hold them accountable for slowing the progress of their own students, then nothing will change. The Education Week article hints at the solution:

"They (states) can also use school sites as hubs to promote community and grassroots involvement in turning around schools. In Newark, N.J., the site of a major state intervention, 9,200 parents became involved in school site planning, Slotnick says."

I will put forth the argument here and now that school sites *must* become hubs of the community. They must not only promote community and grassroots involvement in schools, they must provide training and grassroots involvement in our *communities* and in our *homes*. Dr. Cosby went into our communities and challenged us to raise our children, and not rely on teachers to do so. Schools must issue the same challenge. They must then provide communities with the help and resources they need. School buildings must become more than groups of classrooms. They must become community centers for change.

Until that day, states will keep spending money, and schools will keep spinning their wheels....

What are your thoughts on this?

AND JUSTICE FOR ALL

It is not a far reach to say that all Americans are familiar with the Pledge of Allegiance. The question is, have we as Americans lived up to it?

I pledge allegiance to the flag of the United States of America, and to the republic for which it stands, one nation, under God, indivisible, with liberty and justice for all.

As simple as this pledge is, it is replete with powerful concepts. It is taught to every student in America. It is ingrained in us as a mantra to live by. So why have we struggled so mightily with incorporating it into our dealings with one other?

To wit: many of us are unfamiliar with the case of the youngest person ever executed in the United States. George Stinney, at the age of 14, was sent to the electric chair on June 16, 1944 for the murder of two girls. The entire trial, from jury selection to court proceeding to deliberation to sentencing, took place in *one day*. The defense never cross-examined a witness. The boy's family was not present at the trial, as his father had been summarily fired from his job and the family told to leave town or face retribution. The teenager supposedly confessed after being interviewed by police, yet there were no witnesses to the interview. No transcript of the trial exists.

Read about the George Stinney case here. http://en.wikipedia.org/wiki/George_Stinney

Many people would ask: "Why bring up a story about a boy who suffered injustice in 1944? I didn't partake in this incident, so why should I have any feelings about it?" As a former history teacher, I would answer that we cannot understand our present, nor can we direct our future without fully understanding and learning from our past. We must not forget. If we are a nation that believes in justice for all, then we must be a nation that fights for the rights of a 14 year old, even one long gone, and whose death echoes against our pledge to one another in schoolhouses across America. It is beyond ironic that young George Stinney's life was taken just ten days after fellow Americans landed on the beaches of Normandy to free the world of tyranny. We *must not* forget....

In today's America, we must be truthful to ourselves about who we are and where we come from. If we are to thrive as a community, we must fully embrace a painful past, so that we may reach for a future truly imbued with the concepts of our pledge. Without justice for young George Stinney, even if it comes as late as present day, there is no framework for our pledge. It loses its *raison d'être,* as do we as Americans.

There are those of us who work hard, pay our taxes, vote and fully engage in the American dream. There are Americans whose lives have been so shaped by pain, torture and disconnection from their past that the Dream has become the American Nightmare. And there is no color, culture or gender that fully describes either one.

So what are we going to do about that?

It is a simple pledge, America. Time to live up to it....

SOUTHERN TREES

On September 21, 2011, two men were executed by Southern courts. A Black man, convicted of shooting and killing a White police officer, was executed in Georgia. A White man, convicted of dragging a Black man to death behind a pickup truck, was executed in Texas.

Southern trees bear a strange fruit.

In a powerful parallel ignored by the media, these executions, representing the culmination of legal cases on opposite ends of the racial divide, took place within hours of each other, even though the crimes themselves occurred almost a decade apart.

The current media cycle has focused a large amount of attention on the case of Troy Davis, the Black man convicted of killing police officer Mark MacPhail in Savannah, Georgia on August 19, 1989. Such attention has been generated because seven of the prosecution's original witnesses, who claimed to see Mr. Davis shoot Officer MacPhail during a dispute, recanted their stories. Several of them went so far as to say that they were coerced by the police to bear witness. Given the reasonable doubt generated by their recantations, Americans took to the streets of Georgia to protest Davis' impending execution. When all appeals to stave off the execution failed, Americans stood by helplessly and mourned what appeared, to them at least, to be a gross misapplication of justice. On September 21, 2011, Americans could only hope that justice was served without prejudice.

Read more about it here. http://en.wikipedia.org/wiki/Troy_Davis

On every social media outlet I have access to, I have borne witness to the American anger that is overflowing the levees of jurisprudence. When I read the statement: "Don't be surprised if you see a lot of attitude on the plantation tomorrow," I was saddened at this acute summation of centuries of American strife.

Meanwhile, without any media fanfare, Lawrence Brewer was executed in Texas on the same day. Brewer, a known White supremacist, was convicted along with two other men of dragging James Byrd to his death on June 7, 1998. On that day in Jasper, Texas, Brewer, along with his accomplices, beat Mr. Byrd with bats and other objects, chained him by the ankles to the back of a pickup truck, and dragged him for over two miles on an asphalt road. Mr. Byrd was killed when his body hit the edge of a culvert, severing his right arm and head. The motive? James Byrd was Black. After dumping Mr. Byrd's body in front of an African-American cemetery, the men testified that they went to a barbeque immediately afterwards.

Get the details here. http://en.wikipedia.org/wiki/Murder_of_James_Byrd,_Jr.

Blood on the leaves, and blood at the root.

On June 26, 2011, just a few months before these executions, a Black man, James Anderson, was killed in Jackson, Mississippi when two White teenagers beat him in a parking lot, then deliberately ran him over with a pickup truck. Hinds County District Attorney Robert Shuler Smith stated that Deryl Dedmon and John Aaron Rice, both 18, rejoiced after the attack. According to Smith, Dedmon allegedly called a friend and announced: "I just ran that nigger over."

See article here. http://newsone.com/1368705/black-man-run-over-killed-in-mississippi-hate-crime-da-says/

These crimes were committed at the turn of the 21st Century, and at the dawning of hope created by the election of America's first Black President. The horror reflected in the song "Strange Fruit," written by Abel Meeropol, still reverberates on the American landscape, as evidenced by the first two lines highlighted here. Billie Holliday, singing the song that was first released in 1939, still echoes the pain, anger and frustration felt by Americans almost a century later.

So how do we as a community harvest a different crop borne by Southern trees? I submit we need look no further than the family of James Byrd for the answer.

On a day that national attention was focused on the execution of Troy Davis, the Byrd family sat vigil at the execution of Lawrence Brewer, convicted of taking the life of their brother; their father; their son. Here is what they had to say:

Renee Mullins, Mr. Byrd's oldest daughter:

"The execution doesn't mean that much to me because it's doesn't bring my father back. I want the world to know that I have forgiven him and I don't hate him."

Betty Byrd-Boatner, Mr. Byrd's sister:

"I feel sorry for Brewer because he has so much hate inside of him, and didn't understand how to get (it) out of him and he took the wrong path."

Read more about the Byrd family vigil here. http://www.kiiitv.com/story/15520434/sister-and-daughter-of-james-byrd-jr-held-vigil-to-honor-him

I can only imagine the pain and anguish of Officer MacPhail's family. But I humbly submit that they heed the wisdom of the Byrds, lest we all continue to harvest a bitter crop.

Epilogue:
Connect the Dots...and Broadcast!

Well. Here we are at The Epilogue. I want to first say thank you for taking the time to read Broadcast Your Inner Champion. This book was written to engender an honest, truthful journey of self-discovery (remembrance) in you. So here we go:

Who are you?

Do you answer this question differently at the Epilogue than you did at the Prologue? If so, then you've been directly impacted by this book just as I'd hoped. The purpose of this book is threefold:

1) To get you to answer two very important questions:
   - Who am I?
   - To whom do I belong?
2) To get you to explore your spiritual and cultural connections to everyone else.
3) To get you to broadcast your self-awareness and new found perspective by taking action that positively impacts others.

I'd also like to point out what this book doesn't do:

1) Give you step by step instructions on how to live your life
2) Tell you what religion you should believe in or what you should call God
3) Tell you what political leanings you must have to be "right" or to corner the market on the "truth."

This is, after all, your journey of self-remembrance. Who you are and to whom you belong are very personal concepts that a book can't tell you. You must discover these things for yourself. "Broadcast Your Inner Champion" was written to guide you in that journey, and to remind you that the answers to these questions were already inside you. You were who you were long before the first trauma of this world touched you. This book is also a reminder that you can't answer these questions without context. You are not alone. Who you are is tied into who others were long before you were born. Who you are today will influence the lives of those not yet born.

The ten workshops of The Berlack Method (the ten blog chapters of this book) are placed in specific order from introspection to connection to impact. My life has taught me that in order to focus your impact on others and maximize it you must start with self. You must be clear about why you are who you are, what makes you tick, what is negotiable for you and what is not. You must know your strengths and your weaknesses. You must know your boundaries. As you remember who you are and to whom you belong, you will have fresh insight that will allow you to see that others are on a journey of remembrance as well. That is where the connection begins. The connection continues when your self-awareness becomes the key to putting away your ego. That's true because when you're self-aware you'll find that you don't have to argue with others about their perspectives of you ("You're ugly / You're wrong / You don't follow God the right way"). Letting go of your ego frees you to give permission to others to be who they are, and allows you to focus more on your connections than your differences. Letting go of your ego also allows you to see differences as talking points, and as opportunities to learn.

Finally, with self-awareness and connection comes a realization of your gifts, and your gifts tie you to your purpose. As you discover your purpose, you will find that your life has meaning…and impact. And that, dear readers, is the point.

I should share with you that I was advised early on that I should only focus on one theme. It was pointed out to me that all of the great motivational speakers have laser-like precision in what they address. One talks about fatherhood and only fatherhood. One talks about best business practices. Another one talks only about relationships. I was advised that if a speaker addresses just one topic, then s/he is more likely to be seen as an expert on that topic. I was told as well that audiences get confused if a speaker addresses too many issues.

I must also share with you that I believe that's absolute hogwash. I refuse to insult your intelligence that way. I truly believe that you can walk and chew gum at the same time. I believe that you are aware that a person can be "expert" in more than one thing. I am convinced that you are smart enough to make the connections between disparate themes. I honestly think that you can take distinct concepts such as faith, cultural connection, team building and parenting and weave a single thread through them. And I will not join those who would suggest that the only way I can get you to follow what I'm saying is to hold your hand and walk you in a straight line in only one direction. Your journey is not linear. Your journey is a full circle, and I will engage you in all three hundred and sixty degrees.

My Own Journey

I also want to share with you that this book is not just the product of research and academic prowess. Broadcast Your Inner Champion is very much a reflection of my own journey of self-remembrance. I came to know the order of The Berlack Method themes because that is how I experienced them. Even as I wrote this, my life and my walk with God continued to teach me lessons about who I am, why I am who I am, to whom I belong, my gifts and purpose, my connection to others, and my ability to have an impact.

The Dreams

I became aware of this journey over twenty years ago. I had a series of dreams specifically meant to prepare me for my life's work. In my first dream, I was a little boy running from a man who was chasing me on my old high school campus. I could not see the man, nor did I know why he was chasing me. I saw an old laundry chute door in the basement wall, and jumped in. I fell for what felt like miles, and landed at the bottom of the chute, which lay suspended a few feet above the ground. I looked up to where I jumped in, and it was so far away that it was only a pinprick of light. The man was standing there searching for me, and I somehow knew he couldn't follow. I cut my way through the chute, and landed on the ground.

I found myself in a boathouse. I ran out of the boathouse onto the beach. It was evening, and it felt like an ancient time, thousands of years ago. In the background, faint and barely discernible, yet astoundingly clear, a song was playing. It was unfamiliar to me, and haunting. Amongst the notes of the song, seagulls cawed overhead. As I ran onto the beach, I saw my mother, a young, White woman in a white robe, running with my brothers, who were also White and wearing robes. My mother looked anxious, but in order to keep from frightening us, she pretended that we were playing a game. I could tell, however, that we were running from something, and we were in danger. We entered a rowboat, and rowed out to sea. I could hear the seagulls overhead as we pushed further and further out into a growing storm. As the waves grew stronger, they rocked our little rowboat until it finally overturned, and we all found ourselves in the water. I looked to my right and saw the rocky shoreline of a tiny island. My mother and I both swam to it. As we reached the shore, I looked at my mother's face as she looked back out to sea. She was terrified. I looked out to the waves and saw that my baby brother, only a few months old, was far away from shore and drowning….

Without thinking, I swam out to save my brother. As I got closer, the waves grew higher. I stopped swimming when the wave in front of me rose to some thirty feet high. I looked both left and right and saw that the wave stretched across the entire horizon, and was sure to overtake me. I had to tilt my head as far as I could just to see the top. I was to be overwhelmed. I would not survive. For the first time in the dream, I felt fear. And at the precise moment I felt fear, the entire ocean turned to mud. I could see my brother's feet, and I realized he was stuck face-down in the mire. The mud was thick enough to walk on, and I ran to my brother, pulled him out, and brought him to my mother. We were both so grateful for the miracle God provided, that we both lay prostrate on the rocky shore, crying and thanking Him for saving us. As I lay, I looked up and saw a small golden globe in front of my face, and I remember thinking how odd and out of place that was....

When I awoke, I was shocked at how vivid the dream was. I could see the faces of my mother and brothers in front of me as I lay in bed. They were so clear to me that I knew I would recognize them if I saw them in the street. Laying there in bed, I could still hear the song playing in my head. "What song is that??" Though I didn't recognize it, I somehow knew that I would find the song in my CD collection....

It took over two hours, but I finally found it. It turned out that the song in my head was called "Exile," by Enya, from her album entitled "Watermark." I remembered that the lyrics were listed in the CD sleeve, so I pulled it out, and searched. When I came across the words.... I don't know how to describe what I felt. The lyrics read as if the song was made just for my dream. I read them over and over, the notes playing in my head as I did, and I knew then that I was hearing from God. My eyes fixated on the last stanza, which struck me like a thunderbolt of inner spiritual truth. In an instant, the answers to the questions "Who am I?" and "To whom do I belong?" had brand new meaning:

"Who then can warm my soul?
Who can quell my passion?
Out of these dreams a boat
I will sail home to you."

Still in shock, I told a very good friend of mine, Edgar Davila, about the dream. He suggested that I speak to his mother and her priest about it. I agreed, and met the priest some weeks later in his home. He only spoke Spanish, and had several people with him, including an interpreter. We went into a bedroom of his house, and all sat there as I told them about the dream. The interpreter took his time in a clear effort to reflect precisely what I meant. The priest never said a word, but just looked at me intently.

When I was done, the priest told me that I was very strong spiritually, and that there was a great work for me to do. He also told me that there were others who were spiritually strong who were disturbed at my awakening, and that they would do all they could to stop me. He told me that the woman in the dream was my spiritual mother, and that she was known as "Nuestra Señora de la Caridad del Cobre" (Our Lady of Charity). He then smiled, looked me directly in the eye, and told me that he was my brother. As the interpreter finished saying this, I looked at him in astonishment. I had no idea what he meant. Anticipating my question, the priest told me to turn around.

When I did, I noticed a life-sized statue standing in front of the now-closed door. Because it was positioned behind the door when opened, I didn't see it as I walked in. The first thing I noticed was the woman standing in her white robe. When I looked at her face, I was astounded that I recognized her. It was my mother in the dream. She had a halo about her head, and in her right hand she held a cross. Tucked away in her left arm was my baby brother, the same one I pulled from the mud. His right hand was fixed in the sign of blessing, and in his left hand he held a small globe, the same one I saw on the beach as I lay prostrate praying to God and thanking Him. As my eyes followed the flow of her robes to her feet, I noticed that she was standing on the moon prominent in my dream. Below her, at the base of the statue, was a rowboat tossing in the harsh waves of a storm. In the boat, on either end, were my brothers, both White, and in the middle, praying on his knees, was a little Black boy. When I saw his face, I almost fell out of my chair. It was *me*.

To say that this was the most powerful spiritual moment of my life would be an understatement. It took years for me to accept and fully process what I saw that day....

Some twenty years later, after another series of dreams confirmed for me that it was time to found The Berlack Method and live in my purpose, I received a phone call from a dear friend, Dr. Renee Carr. She told me that she had dreamt of me the night before. Naturally curious, I asked her what the dream was about. She told me that in her dream I had called her, and for some reason, she decided to let my call go to her voicemail. When she reviewed the message, I told her that I was sitting at my table eating a meal from a Chinese restaurant. I told her that I had three meals in front of me, and that each one provided a fortune cookie. Each fortune, when read separately, was meaningless. But when I combined the three together, they formed a message. The message was from God: "I have already planted the seed. All you have to do is water it, and your blessings will come soon."

When I heard these words from Renee over the phone, I almost dropped it in astonishment. I was floored by the fact that God uses us to speak to us, and that He will, on occasion, make Himself completely obvious. I had gotten used to the idea of having my own dreams about purpose, but to get such a clear message from *someone else's* dream was…well…overwhelming.

The last dream I had concerning my purpose made it clear to me that there was no turning back. In my dream I was floating in the air, just above a high rise building. Standing on the roof was some…being. I couldn't see him directly. He was tossing people off the roof, one by one. Each person fell screaming loudly, horrified at their impending deaths, and at the manner in which they would die. I simply floated and watched, emotionally unattached. As the last person was thrown off, they all floated back to the roof. When the last person reached the roof, the entity threw them back off, one by one. This cycle repeated about three or four times. I continued to float, and watch, unimpressed and unbothered.

The last time the people were thrown off, I noticed that there was a huge, exposed exhaust fan spinning furiously on the side of the building. The panicked, falling people were heading straight for it. My initial thought was that they would be cut apart when they hit the fan, and for the first time in the dream, I feared for them. However, as each person hit the fan, they spun off, and floated horizontally in the air. One by one, they hit the fan, spun off, and formed a horizontal line, neither falling nor rising back to the roof. I awoke with a start….

About a week later, I spoke to Renee about the dream. I felt compelled to tell her that I was terrified about my decision to start The Berlack Method. Although I was following God's direction, I was anxious about the tremendous financial burden of starting a new business, especially in such a depressed economic environment. I was falling behind in my bills, (raise your hand if you've ever had to make a decision between lights and food), and I found myself looking backward at the job I left behind. Even though I hated it, my old job paid the bills. I've never forgotten what Renee told me next. She looked me right in the eye, and told me that I was being hypocritical. I was shocked. "What in the world are you talking about?" I asked. Renee replied: "You're telling me about your fear and about your hardships, but your dream is clearly telling you that your gifts and your purpose are not about you. There are people out there waiting for you to help them. How long will you allow your fear to extend their suffering?"

I resolved then and there that I would live the rest of my life using the gifts God has given me to stay in the purpose He's laid out for me. I resolved to believe in the promises He made to me, and to never again chase paychecks as if I'm the one in control.

A Final Word On Faith

Though I've read the Bible from cover to cover, I tell you here and now that I am not a Christian because of any specific chapter or verse. I am a Christian because of my very real and personal walk with God. When I suggest to you that answering the question "to whom do you belong?" is an integral part of your journey, I do not mean to suggest it as an academic exercise. My experience is that my walk with God is *real*, and was the first step in understanding my gifts and my purpose. I would also point out that my experience is a personal one, and by no means suggests what *your* walk should look like. He calls us all in the way in which we'll hear Him. We'll call Him in the way that connects us to Him. I've no need to debate your spiritual walk because I'm clear that we'll all be humbled when we stand together at the final hour.

I've discussed faith on many occasions with a good friend of mine who's Muslim. We share ideas and learn from one another with each conversation. He summed up my thoughts better than I ever could: "People of faith tend to get along." Amen. Ameen. Ashé.

A Purpose Made Manifest

I mentioned earlier that I went through some tough financial times. After founding The Berlack Method, I had to move out of my home and into a rented room because that was all I could afford. I had to place my things in a frat brother's basement for safekeeping. I had the powerfully hurtful experience of walking to the street where I parked my car to find it no longer there, knowing that I could not pay to get it back.

Not only did I suffer financially, but I suffered emotionally as well. I went to bed anxious and unable to sleep. I had nightmares about people in my past that had hurt me. I found myself sitting in my room, isolated, lonely and angry. The only family members I had near me were my two little girls, and I had little means to travel to them. I was always tired. I was always afraid.

These were the things I told Renee when I shared my dream with her. After her stunning reply to me, I re-examined my circumstances. In the middle of all those things, I always had food to eat. I always had a roof over my head. Once, when I needed money to keep the lights on, I happened upon an acquaintance I met only the year before. When she greeted me with "How are you doing?" something told me to *tell* her, and not to reply with a phony "Oh, I'm fine." When I did, she smiled, and told me that she and her fiancé normally tithe by giving to people directly, and that they had been looking for someone to give money to that month. We both saw God at work when she informed me that she and her fiancé would have the money for me the next day. *Yahweh yireh.* My lights stayed on....

Even as I was going through personal hell, I found part-time work at a community center that allowed me to continue my purpose of helping others. I booked engagements with The Berlack Method, allowing me to guide people with their personal development, based on the insights God granted me. In the middle of my strife, I found myself talking to people about self-awareness, faith, attitude and success, spiritual and cultural connection, parenting, relationship building...on and on. It occurred to me that without going through the things I'd experienced, I'd have nothing to say to my audiences. I could *relate* to them when they told me about their struggles. They could see that I'd gone through the same things they had. That sort of understanding and bonding can't be faked. And when that connection is present, workshops like the ones I just described become powerful and real. Day after day workshop participants would tell me in these exact words: *they'd been waiting for me to come along*. They would share with me how something I'd said in a workshop had stayed with them, and helped them deal with situations they later encountered. They would laugh as they told me they could hear me in their heads when they questioned what to do or how to respond to adversity. Time after time I was given messages about how I was making an impact….

On another front, as I struggled, my ex-wife was incredibly supportive, and worked with me so that I could help financially with the girls whenever I could. Given the circumstances, she could have made life very difficult for me, but she took the high road. Though I was not with my girls every day, and though I did not get to spend as much time with them as I would have liked, my time with them was always quality time. My bond with my girls grew stronger all the while.

That bond would manifest in the single most incredible conversation I've ever had in my life. I was sitting at my desk when my daughter Tori, who's thirteen years old, called me. After we greeted each other, she told me that she had something she wanted me to consider. Any father with daughters knows what usually comes after that. I laughed to myself and asked her to continue. She explained to me that her school Principal was retiring and she wanted to know if I would consider applying for the job. I laughed out loud this time and asked her if she would really want her father as her Principal, and remarked that most kids would hate that. What Tori told me next will remain with me forever. She said: "My daddy as Principal? I would *love* it! Daddy, I don't think you see it, but you have a way of talking to people that's soothing. You would get along great with the teachers and the kids would love you. You have a way of disciplining people without shaming them, and getting them to see things in ways they didn't consider before." I was flabbergasted. I stared at the phone, and wondered who was speaking to me. She sounded so grown and mature. So…wise.

I started to cry uncontrollably, and deep within me I felt compelled to confess to her all of my fears, trials and tribulations. I told her about the difficulties I experienced. I told her how sorry I was that I didn't spend more time with her and her sister. I told her about the amazing juxtaposition of my struggles and the help I was giving others. For the first time in our relationship, I felt as if she were the parent and I the child, and I spoke to her in staccato bursts through my tears. After listening to my confession, Tori replied: "Daddy, don't worry. You're just going through the things that will make you stronger. What an incredible gift it is that God has chosen you to do this work." And that was that. I lost it. I put down the phone and cried harder than I had in years. I realized that I was hearing from God through my own daughter.

What Does This All Mean?

I tell you here and now that for me, broadcasting my inner champion is real. I've not just researched concepts, I've lived them. Had I not researched, lived through and addressed each of the topics of this book, I'd have nothing inside me to share with you. So now comes…

Your Challenge

Did you read each chapter with the Chapter Introduction's questions in mind? What did you think about the issues addressed in each theme? Did you change your mind at all as you read through any chapter…or perhaps even within a particular blog? I posed those questions in each introduction because I want you to *think* about how you think, and how you came to think that way.

How, if at all, has your thought process changed? How has what you believe changed? Remember, even with new insight, the journey continues. I can't tell you how many times I've learned a life lesson, only to repeat the lesson because I didn't apply it. And once I applied it, I failed to continuously apply it, backslid into old habits, and had to learn the lesson all over again. And so it has been and will continue to be with you. Even if you had a serious "a ha!" moment while reading about self-awareness, or parenting or team building, you must challenge yourself to reach back in and re-learn the lesson when you slip – and you will. You must continue to connect the dots between your old experiences, the people in your circle and their experiences, the lessons learned from each, your new experiences with new people, and weave a line through it all. You must discover your own path from introspection to connection to impact.

I have to tell you that being a motivational speaker (and now author) brings a lot of pressure. I am, after all, human, and as I just noted, I continually re-learn the very lessons I teach. Even as I wrote this book, I continuously faced challenge after challenge. I spent many days exhorting others to epiphany in my workshops, and spent many nights at home tired and fighting the fear that refused to die. But instead of letting those challenges and those fears stop me, I am writing this book, and sharing what I learned with you. I'm broadcasting my inner champion.

You will also continue to face challenges. In fact, the more you grow, the more challenges you will face, and the more intense they will become. You will get tired. Fear will creep back into your spirit, even after you've beaten it down. You may put this book down filled with the fire to broadcast, only to succumb to the dirt and grime this world will pour over you. So fight. Pick the book back up if you must. Reread. Rethink. Have faith. Connect the dots again and move forward. If you need strength, remember: your challenges and your blessings are not about you.

And now, dear reader, it's time to take the next step. It's time to answer the questions once and for all.

Who are you?

To whom do you belong?

When you answer, *own* your answer. Remember who you are! And finally, bear in mind that there's no point in having this knowledge if it's of no benefit to others.

So…what are you waiting for?

Go ahead!

Broadcast your inner champion.

Thanks & Acknowledgements

I would need to write a new book entirely just to thank all of the people who've had a hand in the creation of "Broadcast Your Inner Champion...." I will do the best I can to acknowledge everyone, but if you do not see your name here, please charge it to my poor mind and not my heart....

I want to first give all glory and praise to God. I don't have the words the express how grateful I am to Him for all He has done for me. He is my parent, my teacher, my guide, my disciplinarian, my encourager, my strength, my protector and my deliverer. Any light you see in me is His, and any lessons I've been blessed enough to teach, were taught to me by Him.

Thank you Ma (Delores Berlack), Grandma (Elise Berlack) and Grandpa (Weston Berlack), for shaping me into the man I am today. I am the reflection of your love, guidance and awareness, and always will be. You taught me how to be a man, how to love, and how to be a Berlack. I am forever grateful.

Thank you Dad (Gilliam Moore). Although God saw fit to call you home before you saw me, you've been with me every day. From the time I can remember, I've felt your spirit with me, just as you promised Ma. Even though I've never seen you in this world, I've never been fatherless. I love you.

Thank you Tori and Chrissy. You are the lights of my life. It amazes me to watch you both grow and mature into the fine young ladies you are becoming. You keep me laughing, you keep me thinking, and you keep me *praying*. You taught me that my life goes on forever through you.

Thank you Frances E. Rogers, my Nana, for being my rock since childhood. If I needed you, you were there, giving boundless love, help, advice, shelter, warmth, energy, encouragement, hugs and love expressed in food that warmed the soul.

Thank you Deon Lynch Berlack, for teaching me tough life lessons, and for being the woman you are to stand by my side and be my friend as I learned them, processed them, and became a better man. We've been through everything together, and here we still stand….

Thank you Cheryl Richardson, my other "Ma," for teaching me about unconditional love and sacrifice. When I think of strength, kindness, love, generosity and womanhood, I think of you. And no, I haven't forgotten the Escalades! *tipping my cup of coffee*

Thank you Corey Armando Wright, for being the best nephew any man could want. Watching you grow into "Mr. Wright" has been my absolute joy and privilege. Our all-day Madden sessions and long, heartfelt conversations will stay with me forever. I may have taught you a thing or two, but I want you to know here and now that you've taught me so much more….

Thank you Tim and Madonna Parker. I love you both more than you'll ever know. You have become my brother and sister by deed. I don't know how I would have made it through the tough times without your warmth, generosity, encouragement, spiritual nourishment and hospitality. Maddie: thanks for the open, honest conversations. Tim: my chessboard and joysticks are always ready….

Thank you Verna Fludd Johnson, my beautiful sister, for pulling "Broadcast…." out of the fire and breathing new life into it. This book would not be possible without you. *Assalamu alaikum wa rahmatullahi wa barakatuh.*

Thank you Lisa Calicchia for being the angel that you are. You remind me that God always sends help when we least expect it.

Thank you Willie Nabors, one of my oldest and dearest friends. Your prayers, insight and spiritual guidance helped me get to where I am today. Here's to Andover.

I also want to thank and acknowledge, in no particular order: The Virginia Berlack Clan, The New York Berlack Clan, The Delgado/Moore Clan, The Rogers/Davis Clan, The Lynch/Lam/Tanner/Richardson Clan, Jay Sparks, ShawnPaul Brown, Edgar Davila, Karen Myrie, Dina Anderson, Dr. Renee Carr, Dr. Diva Verdun, Michelle Fludd Clower, Yvette Fludd, Leslie Greene, Steven Lang, Gloria Darko White, Erica L. Spruill, Dalyn Allen, Cherie Jones, ShaunaMonique Carter, Maria Garrett, Daletha McRae, The Reverend Kevin Slayton, Sr., Kevin McGowan, Larry Perrin, Marvin Bundy, Hannah and Matt (and baby Adalyn, who runs things), Linwood Franklin, Pam Burke, and truly, the list goes on and on….

All of you who've touched my life, you know who you are. Please accept my poor attempt to let you all know that I see you, and know who you are too.

About The Author

A New York native, Steve Berlack is President and Founder of *The Berlack Method, LLC*. He is a well-respected and sought-after motivational speaker and personal development expert offering workshops, keynote addresses and community engagement events for individuals looking to improve their lives, private companies and non-profit organizations looking to train their staffs, and colleges/universities seeking to fulfill their civic missions. Using *The Berlack Method's* workshop series as the framework, Steve effectively weaves together his wide-ranging background in military, public education and non-profit leadership to drive home powerful messages about self-awareness and personal connections to large audiences.

A former television host at BET, Steve has also appeared on *60 Minutes*, in *Ebony Man Magazine* and in *The City Journal*. Presenting from the perspectives of father, executive, Fulbright Scholar and Malik Shabazz Human Rights Institute Scholar, Steve speaks as much from personal experience as he does from research.

Steve holds a Master's Degree in Teaching from Morgan State University. His undergraduate degree in History was earned at The City College of New York, where he graduated Summa Cum Laude. He is a member of Kappa Alpha Psi Fraternity Inc., and has served on the Board of Codman Square Main Street and on the Board of Overseers of the Financial Services Academy/New England College of Finance.

Steve has two beautiful daughters, Victoria and Christina, who keep him young at heart and spiritually well.

Please feel free to visit him at: www.steveberlack.org

- OR-connect with him on Twitter at: www.twitter.com/@sberlack

Facebook: www.facebook.com/steve.berlack

LinkedIn: www.linkedin.com/profile/view?id=82081071&trk=nav_responsive_tab_profile

Sound Off!